THE BOOK OF THE DEAD
ANCIENT EGYPT

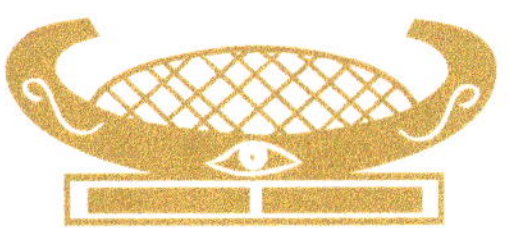

THE BOOK OF THE DEAD
ANCIENT EGYPT

Camelot
EDITORA

I made the judgment of Shu on
that one who knows him, so that I may
go to its cities, and may sail among its
lakes, and walk in Sekhet-Hetepet; and
behold, Ra is in heaven, and behold, the
god Hetep is his double offering. I came to
your land (...) I came so that the gifts that
are about to be given to me may be given,
I rejoice for myself.

President: Paulo Roberto Houch
MTB 0083982/SP

Editorial Coordination: Paola Houch and Priscilla Sipans
Translation: Francine Cervato
English Text Review: Francine Oliveira
Art Coordination: Rubens Martim (cover)
Anthology: Claudio Blanc
Review: Maria Acile Brasil
Review Support: Lilian Rozati
Layout: Jorge Toth
Editorial Production: Vozes do Mundo
Images: cover: Shutterstock; internal pages: Wikicommons

Sales: Phone: +55 (11) 3393-7727 (comercial2@editoraonline.com.br)

The legal deposit was made.

International Data of Cataloging in Publication (CIP)
according to ISDB

C181b   Camelot Editora

    The Book of the Dead Ancient Egypt / Camelot Editora. –
Barueri : Camelot Editora, 2024. 144 p. ; 15,1cm x 23cm.

    ISBN: 978-65-6095-138-9

    1. Religion. 2. Spirituality. 3. Egypt. I. Title.

2024-2549   CDD 200
                                             CDU 2

Elaborated by Vagner Rodolfo da Silva - CRB-8/9410

Rights reserved to
IBC — Instituto Brasileiro de Cultura LTDA
CNPJ 04.207.648/0001-94
Avenida Juruá, 762 — Alphaville Industrial
ZIP CODE. 06455-010 — Barueri/SP
www.editoraonline.com.br

PART I
The Book of the Dead

The goddess Maat

A Hymn to the Setting Sun

A HYMN OF PRAISE TO RA WHEN HE RISES TO THE HORIZON, AND WHEN HE SET IN THE LAND OF LIFE. Osiris, the scribe Ani, said:

Homage to you, oh Ra, when you rise up [as] Tem-Herukhuti (Tem-Harmachis). You are worshiped [by me when] your beauties hover before my eyes and [when your] radiance [falls] over [my] body. You go out on your journey in the boat Sektet with [good] winds, and your heart is happy; the heart of the boat Matet rejoices. You travel the Heavens in peace, and all your enemies are cast down; the stars that never rest sing hymns of praise to you, and the stars that rest and the stars that never fail glorify you as you descend to rest on the horizon of Manu, oh you who are beautiful at dawn and at dusk, oh you Lord who lives and is established, oh my lord!

Homage to you, oh you who are Ra when you rise, and Tem when you set [in] beauty. You rise and shine on the back of your mother [Nut], oh you who are crowned the king of the gods! Nut pays homage to you, and the eternal and unchanging order embraces you morning and night. You walk over heaven, being glad of heart, and the Lake Testes is content [with this]. The demon Sebau fell to the ground; his arms and hands were cut off, and the knife cut the joints of his body. Ra has a good wind; the boat Sektet leaves and, sailing along it, arrives at the port. The gods of the south and the north, of the west and the east, praise you, oh you divine substance, from whom all forms of life arise. You send the word and the earth is flooded with silence.Oh you Only One, who dwelled in heaven before the earth and the mountains appeared. Oh Messenger, oh Lord, oh Only One, you, creator of existing things, you formed the tongue of the company of the gods, you produced everything that comes out of the waters, and you spring from them on the flooded land of the Lake of Horus. Let me inhale the air that comes from your nostrils and the north wind that comes from your mother [Nut]. Oh, make my

A section of folio 3 from the Papyrus of Ani showing the Weighing of the Heart

shining form (khu) glorious, oh Osiris, make my soul (ba) divine! You are worshiped [in] peace (or [in] action), oh Lord of the gods, you are exalted because of your wonderful works. You shine with your rays of light over my body day by day, Osiris the scribe, the teller of the divine offerings of all the gods, the supervisor of the barn of the lords of Abtu (Abydos), the royal scribe, in truth, who loves you; Ani, victorious in peace.

About the Title

"Book of the Dead" is the title commonly given to the great collection of funerary texts that ancient Egyptian scribes composed for the good of the dead. These texts consist of spells and incantations, hymns and litanies, magical formulas and names, words of power and prayers, and these are found engraved or painted on walls of pyramids and tombs, as well as depicted on cof-

A vignette from The Book of the Dead of Ani. The deceased Ani kneels before
Osiris, the judge of the dead

fins, sarcophagi and papyrus scrolls. The title "Book of the Dead" is somewhat unsatisfactory and misleading, as the texts do not form a connected work nor belong to a particular period. They have different characteristics and tell us nothing about the lives and works of the dead with whom they were buried. Furthermore, the Egyptians had many funerary works that could correctly be called "Books of the Dead", but none of them had a name that could be translated. This title was given to the great collection of funerary texts from the early 19th century by early Egyptologists, who did not have exact knowledge of their contents. They were familiar with papyrus scrolls written in hieroglyphic and hieratic characters, as several copies had been published, but the texts in them were short and fragmentary.

The publication of the facsimile[1] from the papyrus of Pcta-Amun-

---

1   Copie Figurée d'un Rouleau de Papyrus trouvé para Thèbes dans un tombeau des Rois. Paris,
    XIII–1805. This papyrus is nearly 30 feet long and was brought to Strasbourg by a paymaster of
    Napoleon's Army in Egypt named Poussielgue, who sold it to M. Cadet.

Neb-Nest-Taui by M. Cadet in 1805 made available for study a long hieroglyphic text and numerous colorful vignettes, and French Egyptologists described it as a copy of "Rituel Funéraire" of the ancient Egyptians. Among these was Champollion le Jeune, who later, on his return from Egypt, he and others called the collection of texts "Le Livre des Morts", "The Book of the Dead", "Das Todtenbuch", and so on. These titles are mere translations of the name given by Egyptian tomb robbers to each scroll of inscribed papyrus that they found with mummies, namely: "Kitâb-al-Mayyit", "Book of the Dead Man", or "Kitâb al- Mayyitun," "Book of the Dead." These people knew nothing about the contents of these scrolls and all they wanted to say was that they were found in the sarcophagus of a dead man.

The Preservation of the Mummified Body in the Tomb by Thoth

The objects found in the graves of pre-dynastic Egyptians, i.e., food vessels, flint knives, and other weapons, etc., prove that these early inhabitants of the Nile Valley believed in some kind of future existence. But as the art of writing was unknown to them, their tombs contained no inscriptions; we can only infer, from texts of the dynastic period, what their ideas about the Other World were. It is clear that they did not consider it of great importance to preserve the dead body in as complete and perfect state as possible, for in many of their graves, the heads, hands, and feet were found separated from the trunks and lying at some distance from them.

On the other hand, the dynastic Egyptians, whether due to differences in religious belief or due to the influence of invaders who established themselves in their country, attached supreme importance to the preservation and integrity of the dead body and adopted all the means known to them to prevent its dismemberment and decay. They cleaned it and embalmed it with drugs, spices and balms; they anointed it with aromatic oils and preservative fluids; they wrapped it in hundreds of meters of linen bandages; and then they sealed it in a coffin or sarcophagus, which they placed in a chamber excavated in the bowels of the mountain. All of these things were done to protect the physical body against dampness, decay, and attacks by moths, beetles, worms, and wild animals. But these were not the only enemies of the dead against which precautions had to be taken, as both the mummified body and the spiritual elements that inhabited it on earth had to be protected from a multitude of genies and demons, as well as from the powers of the darkness in general. These evil powers had horrible and terrifying forms and their haunting were well known, as they infested the region through which the road of the dead passed, which led from this world to the realm of Osiris. The "great gods" were afraid of them and were forced to protect themselves by the use of spells, magical names, and words of power composed and written by Thoth. In fact, it was believed in very ancient times in Egypt that Ra, the Sun God, owed his continued existence to the possession of a secret name which Thoth had given him. And every morning the rising Sun was threatened by a terrible monster called Apep, which hid under the place where the Sun rises, waiting to swallow the solar disk. It was impossible, even for the Sun God, to destroy this "Great Demon." However, by reciting every morning the powerful spell that Thoth had provided him, he was able to paralyze all of Apep's limbs and rise into this world. Since then, the "great gods," although benevolently disposed towards them, were not able to free the deceased from the demons that lived in the "bodies, souls, spirits, shadows and hearts of the dead." Thus, the Egyptians decided to invoke the help of Thoth on behalf of their dead and place them under the protection of his almighty spells. Inspired by Thoth, theologians of ancient Egypt composed a large number of funerary texts that were certainly in general use during the fourth dynasty (around 3700 BC) and that were probably well known during the first dynasty. Thus, throughout the period of dynastic history, Thoth was considered the author of the *Book of the Dead*.

The Book *Per-t Em Hru,* or *[The Chapters of] Coming Forth by (or into) the Day,* Commonly Called *The Book of the Dead*

The spells and other texts written by Thoth for the benefit of the dead and which are directly linked to him were called, according to documents written in the 21st and 28th dynasties, "Chapters of the spells and other texts written by Thoth for the benefit of the dead and which are directly linked to him were called, according to documents written in the 21st and 28th dynasties, "Chapters of the Coming Forth by (or into) the Day." A rubric in the Papyrus of Nu (Brit. Mus. N° 10477) states that the text of the work called "PER-T EM HRU", that is, "Coming Forth (or into) the Day," was discovered by a high official in the foundations of a sanctuary of the god Hennu during the reign of Semti, or Hesepti, a king of the first dynasty. Another rubric on the same papyrus says that the text was engraved on the alabaster pedestal of a statue of Menkaure (Mycerinus), a king of the fourth dynasty, and that the letters were inlaid with lapis lazuli. The pedestal was found by Prince Herutataf, a son of King Khufu (Cheops), who took it to his father and displayed it as a "wonderful" thing. This composition was greatly revered, as it "would make a man victorious on Earth and in the Other World. It would ensure him a safe and free passage through the Tuat (Underworld); it would allow him to enter and leave and take any form he wanted at any time. This would make his soul blossom and prevent him from dying the [second] death." In order for the deceased to receive the full benefit of this text, it had to be recited by a man "who was ceremonially pure, who had not eaten fish or meat and had no relations with women." In the sarcophagi of 11th dynasty and in the papyri of 18th dynasty we find two versions of the PER-T EM HRU, one long and one short, current during the same period. The rubric that attributes

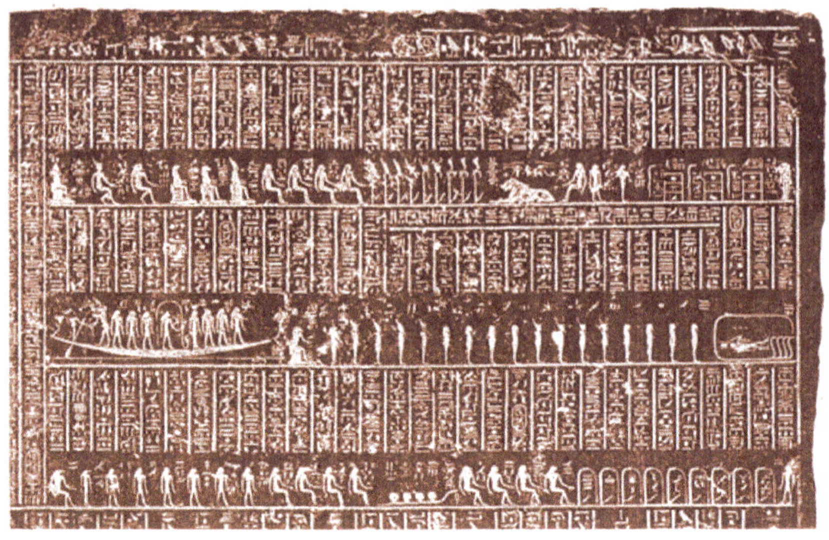

Scenes and texts from the Sixth Section of the *Book of the one that is in the Other World.* From the sarcophagus of King Nekht-Heru-hebt, 378 BC [Southern Egyptian Gallery, Bay 28, N 923].

the "finding" of the chapter to Herutataf associates it with Khmunu, that is, Hermopolis, and indicates that Thoth, the god of this city, was its author. In the Saite Recension, this chapter does not have a vignette, but has the title "Another Chapter of the Chaplet of Victory," and is organized in table form. The words, "Hail, Thoth, make Osiris Auf-ankh, victorious, triumph over his enemies as you made Osiris triumph over his," which are written in two horizontal lines, must be repeated before each column of text. The "great sovereign princes" invoked are: (1) Anu (Heliopolis), (2) Tattu, (3) Sekhem (Letopolis), (4) Pe and Tep, (5) An-arut-f, (6) the double land of Rekhti, (7) Restau, (8) Abtu, (9) the paths of the dead, (10) the plowing festival in Tattu, (11) Kher-aba, (12) Osiris, (13) Heaven and Earth, (14) every god and every goddess. The rubric says:

IF THIS CHAPTER IS RECITED REGULARLY AND ALWAYS BY A MAN WHO PURIFIES HIMSELF IN NATRON WATER, HE WILL LEAVE THE DAY AFTER HE ARRIVES IN THE PORT (that is, HE IS DEAD), AND HE WILL PERFORM ALL THE TRANSFORMATIONS THAT HIS HEART SHOULD DICTATE, AND HE WILL COME OUT OF EVERY FIRE.

The work PER-T EM HRU received many additions over the

centuries and finally, under the 18th dynasty, contained about 190 distinct compositions, or "Chapters." The original forms of many of them can be found in the "Pyramid Texts" (i.e., the funerary compositions engraved on the walls of the chambers and corridors of the pyramids of Kings Unas, Teta, Pepi I Meri-Ra, Merenra and Pepi II in Saqqara), which were written under the fifth and sixth dynasties. The forms that many other chapters had under the 11th and 12th dynasties are well represented by the texts painted on the coffins of Amamu, Sen, and Guatep in the British Museum (N° 6654, 30839, 30841). But it is possible that both and the so-called "Pyramid Texts" all belonged to the work PER-T EM HRU and are excerpts from it. The "Pyramid Texts" have no illustrations, but some of the texts on the coffins of the 11th and 12th dynasties have colorful vignettes, for example, those referring to the region to be traversed by the deceased on the way to the Other World, and the Islands of the Blessed or the Elysian Fields. On the upper margins of the inside of such coffins, there are often two or more rows of colorful drawings of the offerings that during the fifth dynasty were presented to the deceased or its statue during the celebration of "Opening the Mouth" service and the performance of the "Liturgy of Funerary Offerings" ceremonies. During the 18th dynasty, when the use of large rectangular coffins and sarcophagi fell somewhat into disuse, scribes started writing collections of chapters from the PER-T EM HRU on papyrus rolls rather than on sarcophagi. Initially, texts were written in hieroglyphs, most of them in black ink; an attempt was made to illustrate each text with a vignette drawn in black outline. The best -known example of such a codex is the Papyrus of Nebseni (Brit. Mus. N° 9900), which is 77 feet 7½ inches long and 1 foot 1½ inches wide. At the beginning of the 18th dynasty, scribes started writing the titles of the chapter, rubrics and catchwords in red ink and the text in black and it became customary to decorate the vignettes with colors and increase their size and number. The oldest codex of this class is the Papyrus of Nu (Brit. Mus. N° 10477) which is 65 feet 3½ inches long and 1 foot 1½ inches wide. This and many other rolls were written by their owners for their own tombs, and in each roll both the text and the vignettes

Vignette and text from the
Theban Book of the Dead,
from the Papyrus of Nu
[Brit. Mus., N 10477] ,
18th dynasty.

were usually the work of the same hand. Later, however, the scribe wrote only the text and a skilled artist was hired to add the colorful vignettes, whose spaces were marked and left blank by the scribe. The best example of this class of roll is the Papyrus of Ani (Brit. Mus. Nº 10470) which is 78 feet long and one foot three inches wide. In all papyri of this class, the text is written in hieroglyphs, but under the 19th and following dynasties, many papyri are written in hieratic character. These generally lack vignettes but have colorful frontispieces.

Under the rule of the High Priests of Amen, many changes were introduced to the contents of the papyri, and the arrangement of the texts and vignettes of the PER-T EM HRU was altered. The great confraternity of Amun-Ra, the "King of the Gods," thought it was necessary to emphasize the supremacy of their god, even in the realm of Osiris, and added many prayers, litanies, and hymns to the Sun God in each selection of the texts from the PER-T EM HRU, which were copied on papyrus roll for funerary purposes. Most papyrus rolls from this period are short and contain only a few chapters, for example, the Papyrus of the Royal Mother Netchemet (Brit. Mus. N° 10541) and the Papyrus of Queen Netchemet (Brit. Mus. N° 10478). In some, the text is very defective and carelessly written, but the colorful vignettes are remarkable for their size and beauty. The best example of this class of roll is the Papyrus of Anhai (Brit. Mus. N° 10472). The most interesting of all the rolls that were written during the rule of the Priest-Kings over Upper Egypt is the Papyrus of Princess Nesitanebtashru (Brit. Mus. N° 10554), now commonly known as the "Greenfield Papyrus." It is the longest and widest known funerary papyrus, measuring 123 feet by 1 foot 6½ inches, and contains more chapters, hymns, litanies, adorations, and homages to the gods than any other roll. The 87 chapters of the PER-T EM HRU prove the princess' devotion to the cult of Osiris, and the hymns to Amun-Ra show that she considered this god and Osiris not as rivals, but as two aspects of the same deity. She believed that the "hidden" creative power that materialized in Amen was just another form of the power of procreation, renewed birth, and resurrection typified by Osiris. The oldest copies of the PER-T EM HRU that we have on papyrus contain some extracts from other ancient funerary works, such as the "Book of Opening the Mouth," the "Liturgy of Funerary Offerings," and the "Book of the Two Paths". But under the rule of the Priest-Kings, the scribes incorporated the chapters of the PER-T EM HRU extracts from the "Book of Ami-Tuat" and the "Book of Gates," as well as several of the vignettes and texts found on the walls of the royal tombs of Thebes.

One of the most remarkable texts written in this period is found in the Papyrus of Nesi-Khensu, which is now in the Egyptian Museum in Cairo. This is actually a copy of a contract which is declared to have been made between Nesi-Khensu and Amun-Ra, "the holy god, the lord of all gods." As a reward for the great piety of the queen and her devotion to the interests of Amun-Ra on Earth, the god under-

Her-Heru, the first Priest-King, and Queen Netchemet, standing in the Hall of Osiris and praying to the god while the Queen's heart is being weighed in the Scales [Southern Egyptian Gallery, N 758], 21st dynasty, circa 1050 BC.

takes to make her a goddess in his kingdom, to provide her with an estate there in perpetuity, a secure inheritance, supply of offerings, and happiness of heart, soul, and body, and the [daily] recitation of the "Seventy Songs of Ra" for the benefit of her soul in the Khert-Neter, or Underworld. The contract was written in a series of paragraphs using a language similar to that used in the drafting of laws by the priests of Amun, who believed they had the power to make their god do whatever they wanted, whenever they wanted.

Little is known about the history of the PER-T EM HRU after the fall of the priests of Amun and during the period of Nubian rule, but under the kings of 26th dynasty, the Book enjoyed a great vogue. Many

The ceremony of "Opening the Mouth" being performed on the mummy of the royal scribe Hunefer at the door of the tomb [from Brit. Mus., Pap. N 9901].

funerary rolls were written in hieroglyphics and hieratic characters and were decorated with vignettes drawn in black outline. At this time, scribes started writing funerary texts in a demotic style. But men no longer copied long selections from the PER-T EM HRU as they had done under the 18th, 19th, and 20th dynasties, partly because the religious views of the Egyptians had undergone a great change and partly because several Books of the Dead of a more popular character appeared. The cult of Osiris triumphed everywhere, and men preferred the hymns and litanies that dealt with his sufferings, death, and resurrection to the compositions in which the absolute supremacy of Ra and his solar cycle of gods and goddesses was assumed or proclaimed. Thus, in the "Lamentations of Isis," the "Festive Songs of Isis and Nephthys," the "Litanies of Seker," the "Book of Honoring Osiris," etc., the central figure is Osiris, and he alone is considered as the giver of eternal life. The dead were no longer buried with large papyrus rolls filled with chapters of the PER-T EM HRU deposited in their sarcophagi, but with small sheets or strips of papyrus, on which were inscribed the above compositions, or the shorter texts of the "Book of Breathings," the "Book of Traversing Eternity," or the "Book of May My Name Flourish," or a part of the "Chapter of the Last Judgment."

Thoth, the Author of the *Book of the Dead*

Thoth, in Egyptian Tchehuti or Tehuti, who, as already mentioned, is the author of the texts that form the PER-T EM HRU, or *The Book of the Dead*, was considered by the Egyptians as the heart and mind of the Creator, which in very ancient times, in Egypt, was called "Pautti" by the natives, and "Ra" by foreigners. Thoth was also the "tongue" of the Creator and always expressed the will of the great god, as well as pronounced the words that commanded all beings and things in heaven and on

Tehuti (Thoth).

earth to come into existence. His words were almighty, and once uttered, they never remained without effect. He formulated the laws by which heaven, earth, and all celestial bodies are maintained; ordered the courses of the Sun, the Moon and the stars; invented drawing and the arts, the letters of the alphabet; and the art of writing, as well as the science of mathematics. From an early age, he was called the "Scribe (or secretary) of the Great Company

Detail from the Papyrus of Ani.

of the Gods," and because he kept the heavenly record of men's words and actions, he was considered by many generations of Egyptians as the "Recording Angel." He was the inventor of physical and moral Law, and became the personification of JUSTICE. As the Companies of the Gods of Heaven, Earth, and the Other World appointed him to "weigh the words and deeds" of men, and because his verdicts were unalterable, he became more powerful in the Other World than Osiris himself. Osiris owed his triumph over Set in the Great Hall of Judgment of the Gods entirely to the skill of Thoth and his "wise mouth" as an advocate of his cause and his influence with the gods in Heaven. Every follower of Osiris trusted in the advocacy of Thoth to ensure its acquittal on the Day of Judgment and obtain eternal habitation in the Realm of Osiris.

Thoth and Osiris

The Egyptians were not satisfied with the mere possession of the texts of Thoth when their souls were being weighed on the Great Scales in the Judgment Hall of Osiris. They also wanted Thoth to act as their advocate on this terrible occasion and prove their innocence, as he had proved that of Osiris before the great gods in prehistoric times. According to a very ancient Egyptian tradition, the god Osiris, who was originally the god of the principle of the fertility of the Nile, incarnated on Earth as the son of Geb, the god of the earth, and Nut, the goddess of the sky. He had two sisters, Isis and Nephthys, and a brother, Set. Osiris married Isis and Set married Nephthys. Geb placed Osiris on the throne of Egypt, and his rule was good and the nation lived happily and prosperously. Set resented this and was very jealous of his brother. Set wanted to kill Osiris to take his throne and Isis, whose reputation as a devoted and loving wife and capable administrator, spread throughout the country. By some means or another, Set managed to kill Osiris: according to one story, he killed him beside a canal at Netat, near Abydos, and according to another, caused him to be drowned. Isis, accompanied by her sister Nephthys, went to Netat and rescued the body of her lord, and the two sisters, with the help of Anpu, son of Ra, the Sun God, embalmed him. Then they placed the body in a tomb, and a sycamore grew and flourished over the grave. A tradition found in the Pyramid Texts states that before Osiris was placed in his tomb, his wife Isis, by means of her magical powers, managed to temporarily restore him to life and make him bear in her an heir, who came to be called Horus. After the burial of Osiris, Isis withdrew to the marshes of the Delta, and there she gave birth to Horus. In order to avoid persecution from Set, who on one occasion managed to kill Horus with the sting of a scorpion, she fled from place to place in the Delta and lived a very unhappy life for some years. But Thoth helped her in all her difficulties and provided her with the words of power that restored Horus to life and enabled her to pass unharmed among the crocodiles and other evil beasts that infested the waters of the Delta at that time.

When Horus reached maturity, he went in search of Set to wage war against his father's murderer. At last, they met, and a fierce fight ensued, in which, although Set was defeated, before he was finally thrown to the ground, he managed to tear out the right eye of Horus, which he kept with him. Even after this fight, Set managed to persecute Isis again, and Horus was powerless to prevent this. However, Thoth made Set give him the right eye of Horus. Thoth then brought the eye to Horus, replaced it in his face, and, spitting on it, restored his sight. Horus then searched for Osiris' body to resurrect him, and when he found it, he untied the bandages so that Osiris could move his limbs and stand up. Under the direction of Thoth, Horus recited a series of formulas as he presented offerings to Osiris. He, his sons and Anubis performed the ceremonies that opened the mouth, nostrils, eyes and ears of Osiris. He embraced Osiris and thus transferred to him his ka, that is, his own living personality and virility, and gave him his eye, which Thoth had rescued from Set and replaced in his face. As soon as Osiris ate the eye of Horus, he was endowed with a soul and vital power and thus recovered the full use of all his mental faculties, which death had suspended. Immediately, he rose from his bier and became the Lord of the Dead and King of the Underworld. Osiris became the type and symbol of resurrection among the Egyptians of all periods because he was a god who had originally been a mortal and had risen from the dead.

But before Osiris became King of the Underworld, he suffered further persecution from Set. Putting together a number of disconnected hints and brief statements in the texts, it seems quite clear that Osiris appealed to the "Great Gods" to take notice that Set had murdered him, or that Set brought a series of accusations against Osiris. In all events, the "Great Gods" decided to investigate the

Set, the great liar and God of evil.

Horus of Edfu harpooning the Crocodile Set.

Anubis standing next to the bier of the dead.

The Four Sons of Horus: Imsety, Hapi, Duamutef, and Qebehsenuef.

matter. The Greater and Lesser Companies of the Gods met at the heavenly Anu, or Heliopolis, and ordered Osiris to stand up and defend himself against the accusations brought against him by Set. Isis and Nephthys brought him before the gods, and Horus, "the avenger of his father," came to watch the case on behalf of his father, Osiris. Thoth appeared in the Hall of Judgment in his official capacity as "scribe," that is, secretary of the gods, and the hearing of the evidence began. Set seems to have pleaded his own cause and repeated the accusations he had made against Osiris. The defense of Osiris was undertaken by Thoth, who proved to the gods that the accusations brought against Osiris by Set were unfounded, that the statements of Set were lies, and that therefore Set was a liar. The gods accepted Thoth's proof of the innocence of Osiris and the guilt of Set, and ordered Osiris to be considered a Great God and ruled the Realm of the Underworld, and that Set was punished. Thoth convinced them that Osiris was "MAA KHERU," "the one whose word is fair and true," that is, that he had spoken the truth when he gave his testimony, and in texts from all periods, Thoth is often described as S-MAA KHERU ASAR, that is, the one who proved that Osiris was "the one whose word is fair and true." As for Set the Liar, he was captured by the ministers of the Great Gods, who threw him down on his hands and face, and made Osiris ride on his back

The Book of the Dead of Pajuheru, Ptolemaic Period, 3rd to 2nd centuries BC

as a sign of his victory and superiority. After this, Set was tied with ropes like an animal for sacrifice and, in the presence of Thoth, was cut into pieces.

Osiris as Judge of the Dead and King of the Underworld

When Set was destroyed, Osiris left this world for the realm the gods had given him and started reigning over the dead. He was the absolute king of this realm, just as Ra, the Sun God, was the absolute king of the sky. This region of the dead, or Land of the Dead, is called "Tat," or "Tuat," but where the Egyptians thought it was located is not very clear. The original home of the cult of Osiris was in the Delta, in a city that, in historic times, was called Tetu by the Egyptians and Busiris by the Greeks, and it is reasonable to suppose that the Tuat, over which Osiris ruled, was located near this place. Wherever it was, it was not underground, and it was not originally in heaven or even within its limits; but it was located on the borders of the visible world, in the Outer Darkness. The Tuat was not a place of happiness, judging from the description of it in the PER-T EM HRU, or *Book of the Dead*. When Ani, the scribe, arrived there, he said, "What is this that I have come for? There is neither water nor air here, its depth is unfathomable, it is as dark as the darkest night, and men wander here helplessly. A man cannot live here and be satisfied, and he cannot satisfy the cravings of affection" (Chapter CLXXV). In the Tuat there were neither trees nor plants, as it was the "land where nothing grew;" and in primitive times it was a region of destruction and death, a place where the dead rotted and decayed, a place of abomination, horror, terror, and annihilation. But in very ancient times, certainly in the Neolithic Period, the Egyptians believed in some kind of future life and vaguely conceived that the attainment of that life might depend on the way of life that those who hoped to enjoy it led here. The Egyptians "hated death and loved life," and when the belief gained ground among them that Osiris, the God of the Dead, had risen from the dead and had been acquitted by the gods of heaven after a thorough judgment, beyond the power to "make men and women born again" and "renew life" because of his truth and righteousness, they came to consider him as the Judge as well as the God of the Dead. As time goes by, and moral and religious ideas develop among the Egyptians, it becomes certain to them that only those who have satisfied Osiris in his telling the truth and his honest dealings on earth can hope to be admitted into his realm.

When the power of Osiris became predominant in the Underworld and his fame as a fair and upright judge became established among the natives of Lower and Upper Egypt, it was universally believed that after death all men would appear before him in his dreadful Hall of Judgment to receive their reward or their sentence of condemnation. The writers of the Pyramid Texts, more than fifty-five centuries ago, dreamed of a time when Heaven, Earth, and men did not exist, when the gods had not yet been born, when death had not been created, and when anger, speech, curses, and rebellion were unknown. But that time was very remote, and long before the great fight between Horus and Set, when the former lost his eye and the latter, part of his body. Meanwhile, death came into the world, and as the religion of Osiris gave man a hope of escape from death and the promise of eternal life of the peculiar kind that attracted the great mass of the Egyptian people, the spread of the cult of Osiris and its final triumph over all forms of religion in Egypt was assured. Under the early dynasties, the priesthood of Anu (the On of the Bible) strove to make its Sun God Ra pre-eminent in Egypt, but the cult of this god never attracted the people as a whole. It was embraced by the pharaohs, their high officials, some nobles, and the official priesthood, but the reward its doctrine offered was not popular among materialistic Egyptians. A life spent in the Boat of Ra with the gods, being clothed in light and fed with light, did not attract the common people, since Osiris offered them as a reward a life in the Field of Reeds, the Field of Food Offerings, and the Field of the Grasshoppers, and eternal existence in a transmuted and beautified body among the resurrected bodies of father and mother, wife and children, relatives and friends.

But according to the cult of Ra, the wicked, the rebels, and the blasphemers of the Sun God suffered swift and final punishment, as did all those who sinned against the severe moral Law of Osiris and who failed to satisfy its demands, paid the fine without delay. The Judgment of Ra was held at sunrise, and the wicked were thrown into deep pits filled with fire, and their bodies, souls, shadows, and hearts were immediately consumed. The Judgment of Osiris took place near Abydos, probably at midnight, and a decree of swift annihilation was passed by him on the condemned. Their heads were cut off by the executioner of Osiris, who was called Shesmu, and their bodies were dismembered and destroyed in pits of fire. There was no eternal punishment for men, as the wicked were quickly and completely annihilated; but since Osiris sat in judgment and condemned the wicked to destruction daily, the infliction of punishment never ceased.

The Judgment of Osiris

The oldest religious texts suggest that the Egyptians always associated the Last Judgment with the weighing of the heart on the scales, and in the illustrated papyri of the Book of the Dead, great emphasis is always given to the vignettes in which this weighing is being done. The heart, ab, was taken as the symbol of all emotions, desires and passions, good and bad, and from it come the questions of life. It was closely linked to the ka, that is, the double or personality of a man, and several short spells in the Book PER-T EM HRU were composed to ensure its preservation (Chapters XXVI- XXXB*). The great Chapter of the Judgment of Osiris (Chapter CXXV), is divided into three parts, which are sometimes (as in the Papyrus of Ani) prefaced by a Hymn to Osiris. The first part contains the following, which was said by the deceased when he entered the Hall of Maat, in which Osiris sat to judge:

"Homage to you, oh Great God, Lord of Maat, I came to you, oh my Lord, that I may behold your beneficence. I know you, and I know your name, and the names of the Forty-Two who live with you in the Hall of Maat, who keep sinners and feed on their blood on the day of judging characters before Un-Nefer... I destroyed sin for you. I did not sin against men. I did not oppress [my] relatives. I did not do anything wrong in the place of truth. I did not meet useless people. I did not do any harm. I did not defraud the oppressed of his goods. I did not do the things that the gods abhor. I did not vilify a servant of his master. I did not cause pain. I did not let any man go hungry. I did not make anyone cry. I did not commit murder. I did not order anyone to commit murder for me. I did not inflict pain on anyone. I did not defraud the temples of their oblations. I did not steal the cakes of the gods. I did not steal the offerings from the spirits (i.e., the dead). I did not commit fornication. I did not pollute myself in the holy places of the god of my city. I did not decrease the bushel. I did not take away or add to the acre measurement. I did not invade [others'] fields. I did not add to the weights of the scales. I did not misread the pointer on the scales. I did not take milk out of the children's mouths. I did not drive the cattle from their pastures. I did not trap the birds of the gods. I did not catch fish [with bait made from] fish of its kind. I did not stop the water [when it should flow]. I did not cut a canal dam. I did not extinguish a fire when it should have burned. I did not change the times of the chosen meat offerings. I did not reject the cattle [intended for] offerings. I did not repel the god in his appearances. I am pure. I am pure. I am pure. I am pure..."

In the second part of Chapter CXXV, Osiris is seen seated at one end of the Hall of Maat accompanied by the two goddesses of Law and Truth, and the 42 gods who are there to assist him. Each of the 42 gods represent one of the names of Egypt and has a symbolic name. When the deceased repeated the magical names of the doors of the Hall, he entered and saw these gods arranged in two rows, twenty-one on each side of the Hall. At the end, near Osiris, were the Great Scales, under the command of Anubis, and the monster Ammit, the Eater of the Dead, that is, of the hearts of the wicked who were condemned in the Judgment of Osiris. The deceased advanced through the Hall and, addressing each of the 42 gods by name, declared that it had not committed a particular sin:

"Oh Usekh Nemmat, coming from Anu, I did not commit sin.

"Oh Fenti, coming from Khmunu, I did not steal.

"Oh Neha Her, coming from Re-stau, I did not kill men.

"Oh Neba, coming in retreat, I did not plunder the property of a god.

"Oh Set Qesu, coming from Hensu, I did not lie.

"Oh Uamemti, coming from Khebt, I did not defile any man's wife.

"Oh Ma Antef, coming from Per-Menu, I did not defile myself.

"Oh Tem-Sepu, coming from Tattu, I did not curse the king.

"Oh Nefertum, coming from Het-ka-Ptah, I did not act deceitfully; I did not commit evil.

"Oh Nekhen, coming from Heqat, I did not turn a deaf ear to the words of the Law (or Truth)."

The names of most of the 42 gods are not ancient, but were invented by the priests probably at the same time as the names in the Book of Him that is in the Tuat and the Book of Gates, that is, between the 12th and 18th dynasties. Its artificial character is shown by its meanings. Thus, Usekh Nemmat means "He of the long strides"; Fenti means "He of the Nose;" Neha Her means "Stinking limbs;"

The *Book of the Dead* of Pajuheru, Ptolemaic Period, 3rd to 2nd centuries BC.

Set Qesu means "Bonebreaker," etc. Early Egyptologists called the second part of Chapter CXXV the "Negative Confession," and it is generally known by this somewhat inaccurate title to this day. In the third part of Chapter CXXV comes the speech that the deceased made to the gods after declaring its innocence of the enumerated sins before the 42 gods. It says: "Homage to you, oh gods who dwell in the Hall of Maat. I know you and I know your names. Do not let me fall under your slaughtering knives. Do not bring my wickedness to the knowledge of the god whose followers you are. Do not let the matter [of my judgment] fall under his jurisdiction. Speak the Law (or truth) concerning me before Neb-er-tcher, for I executed the Law (or truth) in Tama-Re (i.e., Egypt). I did not blaspheme against any god. No matter of mine came to the king's attention in his day. Homage to you, oh you who are in the Hall of Maat, who have no lies in your bodies, who live in the truth, who eat the truth before Horus, the dweller of his disk, deliver me from Babai who lives in the bowels of the mighty on the day of the Great Judgment (APT AAT). Here I am! I came to you without sin, without deceit, without evil, without false testimony. I did not do any harm. I live by the truth and I feed on the truth. I fulfilled the commands of men, and the things that satisfy the gods. I pleased a god by [doing] his will. I gave bread to the hungry, water to the thirsty, clothes to the naked, and a boat to the needy. I made sacred offerings to the gods and sepulchral offerings to the beautified dead. So be my saviors, be my protectors, and do not make any accusation against me before the Great God. I am pure in mouth and clean in hands; therefore, it was said by those who saw me, 'Come in peace, come in peace.'"

The deceased then addresses Osiris and says: "Hail, you who are exalted on your standard, you, Lord of the Crown of Atefu, whose name is 'Lord of the Winds', save me from your Messengers (or Advisors) with uncovered faces, who accuses evil and makes sins clear, because I practiced the Law (or Truth) for the Lord of the Law (or Truth). I purified myself with washing in water, my back was cleansed with salt, and my inner parts are in the pool of truth. There is not a limb of mine that lacks the truth." From the lines that follow above in the Papyrus of Nu, it seems that the judgment of the deceased by the 42 gods was preliminary to the final judgment of Osiris. In any case, after questioning it about the performance of certain ceremonies, they invited it to enter the Hall of Maat, but when it was about to do so, the gatekeeper, and the bolts of the door, and the several parts of the door and its frame and floor refused to allow it to enter until it repeated their magical names. After pronouncing them correctly, the gatekeeper welcomed the deceased and introduced it to Maau-Taui, who was Thoth himself. When asked by him why he had come, the deceased answered, "I came so that the report may be made of me." Then Thoth said, "What is your condition?" And the deceased replied, "I am purified from evil things, I am free from the evil of those who lived in my days; I am not one of them." Regarding this, Thoth said, "You will be evaluated. [Tell me:] Who is the one whose roof is fire, whose walls are living serpents, and whose floor is a stream of water? Who is he?" The deceased answered, "Osiris." Thoth then led him to the god Osiris, who received it, and promised that subsistence should be provided for it from the Eye of Ra.

In large papyri of the Book of the Dead, such as those of Nebseni, Nu, Ani, Hunefer, etc., the Last Judgment, or the "Great Reckoning," is the most prominent scene in the entire work, and the vignette, in which is depicted is several feet long. The most complete form

The *Book of the Dead* of the Egyptian adviser Yuya, 14th century BC.

The weighing of the heart of the Scribe Ani on the Great Scales in the Hall of Osiris [from the Papyrus of Ani, Brit. Mus., Pap. N 10470].

is given in the Papyrus of Ani and may be thus described: at one end of the Hall of Maat, Osiris is seated on a throne within a sanctuary made in the form of a funerary vault; behind him are Isis and Nephthys. Along one side of the Hall are seated the gods Harmachis, Tem, Shu, Tefnut, Geb, Nut, Horus, Hathor, Hu and Saa, who are to serve as the divine jury; these formed the "Great Company of the Gods" of Anu (Heliopolis). Beside them are the Great Scales, and on their pillar is the dog-headed ape Astes, or Astenu, the associate of Thoth. The pointer of the scales is in charge of Anpu. Behind Anpu are Thoth, the scribe of the gods, and the monster Ammit, with the head of a crocodile, the front paws and shoulders of a lion, and the hindquarters of a hippopotamus; the duty of the last was to devour the hearts that were heavy on the Scales. On the other side of the Scales, Ani, accompanied by his wife, is seen standing with his head bowed in worship, and between him and the scales are the two nursing and child-rearing goddesses, Meskhenet and Rennet, the soul of Ani, in the form of a falcon with a man's head and his consort Shai. As the heart was considered the seat of all will, emotion, feeling, reason, and intelligence, Ani's heart is seen in one part of the Scales, and in the other is the feather, a symbol of truth and righteousness. While his heart was on the scales, Ani, repeating the words of Chapter XXXB* of the Book of the Dead, addressed him, saying: "My heart of my mother! My heart of my mother! My heart of my being! When testifying against me, do not push me back before the Tchatchaut (i.e., the supervisors of Osiris), and do not fail regarding me before the Master of the Scales. You are my ka, the dweller in my body, uniting and strengthening my limbs. You will come towards the happiness to which we advance. Do not make my name stink before the officials [of Osiris], do not speak lies against me before the Great God, the Lord of Amenti."

Then Thoth, the Judge of Truth, of the Great Company of the Gods who are in the presence of Osiris, said to the gods: "Hear this word: verily the heart of Osiris was weighed, and his soul bore testimony concerning him; according to the Great Scales, his case is true (i.e., fair). No evil was found in him. He did not steal offerings from the temples. He did not act dishonestly and did not defame people when he was on earth."

And the Great Company of the Gods says to Thoth, who lives in Khmunu (Hermopolis): "That which comes out of your mouth of truth is confirmed; Osiris, the scribe Ani, true in voice, testified.

Horus, Son of Isis, presenting the Scribe Ani to Osiris [from the Papyrus of Ani, Brit. Mus., Pap. N 10470].

He did not sin and [his name] does not smell bad before us; Ammit (that is, the Devourer of the Dead) will not have dominion over him. May be given to him offerings of food and an appearance before Osiris, and a permanent property in the Field of Offerings as the Followers of Horus."

Thus, the gods declared that Ani is "true of voice," as was Osiris, and they called Ani "Osiris," because in his purity of word and deed he resembled that god. In all copies of the Book of the Dead the deceased is always called "Osiris," and as it was always assumed that those for whom they were written would be considered innocent when weighed on the Great Scales, the "true of voice" words, which were equivalent in meaning to "innocent and acquitted," were always written after their names. It may be noted in passing that when Ani's heart was weighed against the Truth, the beam of the Great Scales remained perfectly horizontal. This suggests that the gods did not expect the deceased's heart to "kick the beam," but they were quite pleased if this exactly counterbalanced the Truth. They demanded the fulfillment of the Law and nothing more, and were content to grant immortality to the man to whom Thoth's verdict was "he did no harm".

According to the command of the gods, Ani passes from the Great Scales to the end of the Hall of Maat where Osiris is seated, and when he approaches the god Horus, the son of Isis takes him by the hand and leads him forward, and standing before his father Osiris, says: "I came to you, Un-Nefer, I brought to you Osiris Ani. His heart is fair [and] came out of the Scales. He has no sin before any god or any goddess. Thoth established his written judgment, and the Company of the Gods declared on his behalf that [his] evidence is very true. May be given to him the bread and beer that appear before Osiris. May he be like the Followers of Horus forever!" We then see Ani kneeling in worship before Osiris, and he says: "Behold, I am in your presence, oh Lord of Amenti. There is no sin in my body. I did not knowingly utter a lie. [I have] no duplicity. Grant that I may be like the favored (or rewarded) who are in your wake." Under the favor of Osiris, Ani then became a sahu, or "spirit-body," and passed into the Realm of Osiris.

The Realm of Osiris

According to the Book of Gates and the other "Guides" to the Egyptian Underworld, the Realm of Osiris formed the Sixth Division of the Tuat; in very ancient times, it was located in the Western Delta, but after the 12th dynasty. Theologians placed it near Abydos in Upper Egypt, and before the end of the Dynastic Period, the Tuat of Osiris had absorbed the Underworld of all nomes of Egypt. When the soul, in its beauty or spiritual body, arrived there, the ministers of Osiris took it to the property or place of residence assigned to it by Osiris' command, and there started its new existence. The great vignette in Chapter XX shows us exactly what kind of place the abode of the blessed was. The country was flat and the fields were crossed by canals of running water in which there were "no fish or worms" (that is, water snakes). In one part of it there were several small islands, and on one of them Osiris was supposed to live with his gods. It was called the "Island of Truth," and the boatman of Osiris would bring him no soul that had not been declared "true in words" by Thoth, Osiris, and the Great Gods in the "Great Reckoning." The portion of the Realm of Osiris depicted in the great Books of the Dead represents, in many aspects, a typical Egyptian farm, and we see the deceased engaged in plowing, harvesting, and driving the oxen that are treading the corn. He was introduced into the Sekhet-Hetepet (a section of the Sekhet-Aaru, i.e., "Field of Reeds," or the "Elysian Fields") by Thoth, and there he found the souls of his ancestors, who joined the company of the gods. A corner of this region was specially set aside for the abode of the aakhu, that is, beautified souls, or spiritual souls, which were said to be seven cubits high, and for harvesting wheat or barley that grew to a height of three cubits. Near this place, two boats were moored and these were always ready for the use of the inhabitants of that region; they seem to have been "spiritual boats," that is, boats that moved by themselves and took the beautified ones wherever they wanted to go without any trouble or fatigue on their part.

How the beautified ones spent their time in the Realm of Osiris can be seen in the images engraved in the alabaster sarcophagus of Seti I, now preserved in Sir John Soane's Museum in Lincoln's Inn Fields. Here we see them busy producing the heavenly food on which they and the god lived. Some are tending the wheat plants as they grow, and others are harvesting the ripe grains. In the texts accompanying these scenes, it is said that the ears of wheat are the "limbs of Osiris," and the wheat plant is called the Maat plant. Osiris was the god of wheat and the personification of Maat (i.e., the Truth), and the beautified ones lived upon the body of their god and ate it daily. The substance of it was the "Bread of Eternity," which is mentioned in the Pyramid Texts. The beautified ones are described as "those who offered incense to the gods, and whose kau (i.e., doubles, or people) were washed. They were counted and are maat (i.e., Truth) in the presence of the Great God who destroys sin". Osiris says to them: "You are the truth of the truth; rest in peace."

And about them, he says: "They were doers of the truth while

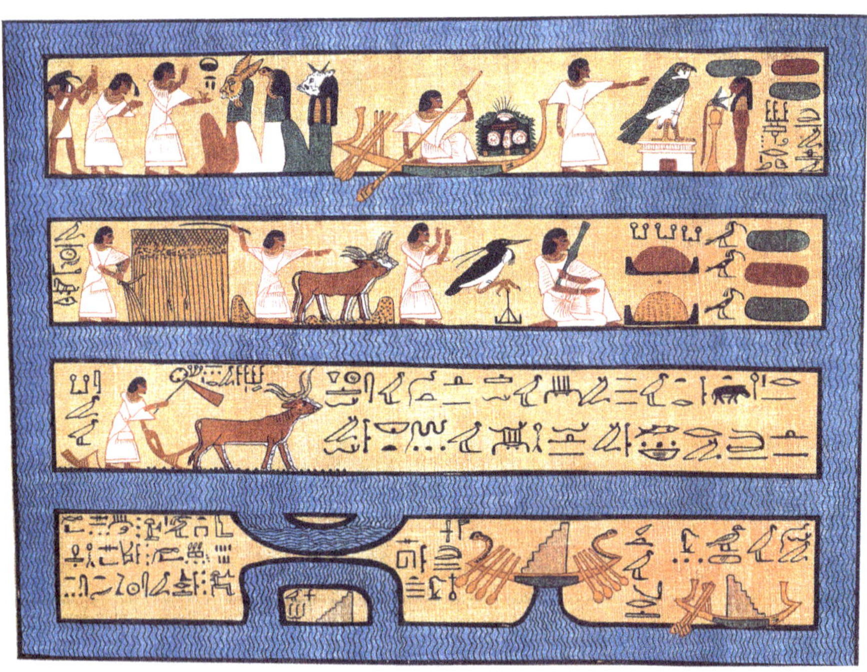

The Elysian Fields of the Egyptians [from the Papyrus of Ani, Brit. Mus., Pap. N 10470].

on earth, they fought for their god, and they will be called to the enjoyment of the Land of the House of Life with Truth. Their truth will be told to them in the presence of the Great God who destroys sin." Then, addressing them again, Osiris says: "You are beings of Truth, oh truths. Rest because of what you did, becoming like those who follow me, and who rule the House of The One whose soul is holy... You will live there as they live and will have dominion over the cool waters of their land. I command you to have your being to the limit [of that land] with Truth and without sin." In these excerpts, we have the two conceptions of Osiris well illustrated. As the god of wheat, he would satisfy those who wanted a purely material, agricultural heaven, where hunger was unknown and where the blessed could satisfy every physical want and need on a daily basis; and as the God of Truth, of whom the spiritual mind hoped to become the counterpart, he would be their hope, consolation, and image of the Eternal God.

A Brief Description of the "Doors" or Chapters of the *Book of the Dead*

All the great papyri of the *Book of the Dead* begin with a HYMN TO RA, who, from the period of the fourth dynasty, was the "King of the Gods" of Egypt. His cult was finally "established" under the fifth dynasty when the king of Egypt started calling himself in official documents and monuments "Son of the Sun," Sa Ra. This Hymn must be sung by the deceased. It says: "Homage to you, oh Ra, in your beautiful birth. You rise, you rise; you shine, you shine at dawn. You are the King of the Gods, and the goddess Maat embraces you. The Company of Gods praises you at sunrise and sunset. You sail on the heights of the sky and your heart is happy. Your Morning Boat meets your Night Boat with fair winds. Your father is the Sky-God and your mother is the Sky-Goddess, and you are Horus of the Eastern and Western Skies... Oh, you Only One, oh, you Perfect One, oh, you who are eternal, who are never weak, who no one can lower; no one has dominion over the things that belong to you. Homage to you in your characters of Horus, Tem, and Khepera, you, Great Falcon, who makes man rejoice by your beautiful face. When you are resurrected, men and women live. You renew your youth and put yourself in the place where you were yesterday. Oh, divine youth, who created you, I cannot understand you. You are the Lord of heaven and earth, and you created heavenly beings and earthly beings. You are the One God, who came into being at the beginning of time. You created earth and man, you made the sky and the heavenly river Hep; you made the waters and gave life to everything in them. You bound the mountains, created humanity and the wild animals, and made heaven and earth. The demon Nak is knocked down, its arms are cut off. Oh, you, divine youth, heir of eternity, self-begotten and self-born, the Only One, Mighty One, of myriads of forms and aspects, Prince of An (i.e., On), Lord of Eternity, Eternal Ruler, the Company of the Gods rejoice in you. As you rise, you become greater: your rays are on every face. You are unknowable, and no language can describe your likeness; you exist alone. Millions of years went by over the world, I cannot tell the number of those you have passed through. You travel through the spaces [requiring] millions of years [to pass] in a small moment of time, and then you establish and make the end of the hours."

The subject of the extract is treated in more detail in Chapter XV, which contains a long Hymn to Ra in his rising, or Amun-Ra, or Ra united with other sun-gods, for example, Horus and Khepera, and a short Hymn to Ra in his setting. In the latter, the welcome that Ra receives from the inhabitants of Amenti (that is, the Hidden Place, like the Greek "Hades") is emphasized as follows:

"All the beautified dead (aakhu) in the Tuat welcome him to the horizon of Amenti. They shout praise to him in his form of Tem (that is, the setting sun). You rose and became strong, and established yourself, a living being, and your glories are in Amenti. The gods of Amenti rejoice in your beauty (or beneficence). The hidden ones worship you, the elders bring you offerings and protect you. The souls of Amenti cry out, and when they meet Your

Majesty (Life, Strength, Health be to you!) they shout 'Hail! Hail!' The lords of the mansions of the Tuat reach out their hands to you from their abodes, and they cry to you, and follow in your shining entourage, and the hearts of the lords of the Tuat rejoice when you send your light to Amenti. Their eyes follow you; they move forward to see you, and their hearts rejoice at the sight of your face. You answer the supplication of those in their graves, dispel their helplessness and drive away evil from them. You give breath. You are greatly feared, your form is majestic, and you are much loved by those who dwell in the Other World."

The Introductory Hymn to Ra is followed by a Hymn to Osiris, in which the deceased says: "Glory to you, oh Osiris Un-Nefer, you, great god in Abtu (Abydos), King of Eternity, Lord of Eternity, God whose existence is millions of years old, the eldest son of Nut, begotten by Geb, the Ancestor-Chief, Lord of the Southern and Northern Crowns, Lord of the High White Crown. You are the Governor of gods, and men and you received the scepter, the whip and the rank from your Divine Parents. Leave your heart in Amenti and be glad, for your son Horus is seated on your throne. You are Lord of Tetu (Busiris) and Governor of Abtu (Abydos). You make the Two Lands (that is, all of Egypt) fertile by [your] true word before the Lord to the utmost limit... Your power is widespread, and great is the terror of your name, 'Osiris.' You endure for all eternity in your name of 'Un-Nefer' (that is, Beneficent Being). Homage to you, King of kings, Lord of lords, Governor of governors, who from the womb of the Goddess of Sky ruled the World and the Underworld. Your limbs are like silvery gold, your hand is blue like lapis lazuli, and the space on each side of you is the color of turquoise (or emerald). Your body is omnipresent, oh inhabitant of the Land of Holiness, your face is beautiful... The gods come before you, bowing down. They hold you in fear. They withdraw and retreat when they see the horror of Ra upon you; the [thought] of your Majesty's achievements is in their hearts. Life is with you.

Let me follow Your Majesty as when I was on earth, may my soul

The Book of the Dead of the Egyptian adviser Yuya, 14th century BC.

be summoned, and may it be found near the Lords of the Truth. I came to the City of God, the region that is eternally ancient, with my soul (ba), double (ka) and soul-spirit (aakhu), to be an inhabitant in this land. Your God is the Lord of the Truth... I n the last abundant equipment for the tomb and burial in the Land of Holiness. I came to you, my hands hold the Truth, and there is no falsehood in my heart... You put the Truth before you: I know in what you live. I did not commit a sin on this earth; I did not defraud any man of his possessions" (Chapter CLXXXIII).

Chapter I was recited by the priest, who accompanied the mummy to the tomb and performed the funeral ceremonies there. In it, the priest (kher heb) assumed the character of Thoth and promised the deceased to do for it all that it had done for Osiris in the old days. Chapter IB gave the sahu, or "spiritual body," the power to enter the Tuat immediately after the burial of the material body and freed it from the Nine Worms that lived on the dead. Chapters II–IV are short spells written to give the deceased the power to revisit the earth, join the gods, and travel the sky. Chapters V and VI provide for the carrying out of agricultural work in the Other World. The text of chapter VI was cut on figures (call "shabti") made of stone, wood, etc., which were placed in the tomb, and when the deceased recited it, these figures came to life and did whatever the deceased wanted. The shabti took the place of the human funerary sacrifice that was common throughout Egypt before the general adoption of the cult of Osiris under the 12th dynasty. Around 700 shabti were found in the tomb of Seti I, and many of them are in the British Museum.

Chapter VII is a spell to destroy the Great Serpent Apep, the archenemy of Horus the Elder, Ra, Osiris, Horus son of Isis, and all the followers of Osiris. Chapters VIII and IX granted passage for the deceased through the Tuat, and chapters X and XI gave it power over the enemies that are found there. Chapters XII and XIII gave it great freedom of movement in the realm of Osiris. Chapter XIV is a prayer in which Osiris is begged to remove any feelings of dissatisfaction he may have for the deceased, and says: "Wash away my sins, Lord of the Truth; destroy my transgressions, wickedness, and iniquity, oh God of the Truth. May this god be at peace with me. Destroy the things that are obstacles between us. Give me peace and remove all dissatisfaction from your heart in respect of me." Chapter XV has several forms, and each of them contains Hymns to Ra, which were sung daily in the morning and evening; examples of paragraphs are given above. Chapter XVI is just a vignette that illustrates chapter XV; chapter XVII is a very important chapter, as it contains statements of divine doctrine as understood by the priests of Heliopolis. The opening words are: "I am Tem in rising. I am the Only One. I came into existence in Nu (the Sky). I am Ra, who rose again in primeval time, ruler of what he had made." After that comes the question: "Who is this?" and the answer is: "It is Ra who rose in the city of Hensu, in the primeval time, crowned as king. He existed in the height of the Dweller in Khmunu (that is, Thoth of Hermopolis) before the pillars that support the sky were made." Chapter XVIII contains the Speeches to Thoth, in which it is supplicated that the deceased is declared innocent before the gods of Heliopolis, Busiris, Letopolis, Mendes, Abydos, etc. These speeches formed a very powerful spell, which was used by Horus, and when he recited it four times, all his enemies were overthrown and cut to pieces.

Chapters XIX and XX are variant forms of Chapter XVIII. Chapters XXI to XXIII grant Thoth's help in "opening the mouth" of the deceased, where by he obtained the power to breathe, think, drink, and eat. Thoth recited spells on the gods while Ptah untied the bandages, and Shu forced open their mouths with an iron knife. Chapter XXIV gave the deceased a knowledge of the "words of power" (hekau) that were used by the great god Tem-Khepera, and Chapter XXV restored its memory. Five chapters, from XXV to XXX, contain prayers and spells by which the deceased obtained power over his heart and gained absolute possession of it. The most popular prayer is that of Chapter XXXB which, according to its rubric, was "found," that is, edited by Herutataf, son of the great Cheops, around 3600 BC. This prayer was still in use in the early years of the Christian Era. In the Papyrus of Nu, it is associated with Chapter LXIV, and the oldest form probably existed under the first dynasty.

Chapters XXXI to XLII were written to free the deceased from the Great Crocodile Sui, and the Serpents Rerek and Seksek, and the Lynx with its deadly claws, and the Beetle Apshait, and the terrible serpent goddess Meretseger, and a group of three particularly poisonous serpents, and Apep, a personification of Set, the god of evil, and the Eater of the Ass, and a series of beings who lived by killing the souls of the dead. In Chapter XLII, each limb of the deceased is placed under the protection of, or identified with, a god or goddess, e.g., the hair with Nu, the face with Aten (that is, the solar disk), the eyes with Hathor, and the deceased exclaims triumphantly: "There is no limb of my body that is not the limb of a god." In chapter XLIII, a spell to prevent the decapitation of the deceased, which assumes the character of Osiris, the Lord of Eternity. In chapter XLIV, an ancient and powerful spell, which recitation prevented the deceased from dying a second time. Chapters XLV and XLVI preserved the deceased's mummy from decomposition, and chapter XLVII prevented the removal of his seat or throne.

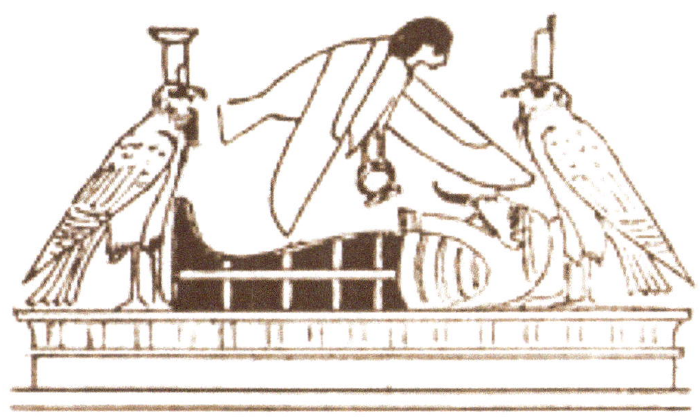

The soul visiting the mummified body in the tomb. The Bird- Goddess on the head is Isis, and on the feet is Nephthys.

Chapter L allowed the deceased to avoid blocking the execution of the god Shesmu. Chapters LI to LIII provided the deceased with pure food and clean water from the table of the gods; he lived by what they lived and, thus, became one with them. Chapters LIV to LXII gave the deceased the power to obtain cool water from the Heavenly Nile and the water sources of heaven, and being identified with Shu, the god of light and air, it was able to pass through the entire earth at will. Its life was that of the Egg of the "Great Cackler," and the goddess Sesheta built a house for it in the Heavenly Anu, or Heliopolis.

The recitation of chapter LXIII allowed the deceased to avoid drinking boiling water in the Tuat. The water in some of its lakes was cool and refreshing to those who told the truth, but it turned to boiling water and scalded the wicked when they tried to drink from it. Chapter LXIV is the epitome of the entire *Book of the Dead*, and forms a "great and divine protection" for the deceased. The text is mystical in character and suggests that the deceased could, through its recitation, absorb the gods into its being, or become absorbed by them itself. Its rubric commands those who recite it to abstain from meat, fish, and women. Chapter LXV gave the deceased victory over all its enemies, and chapters LXVI and LXVII gave it access to the Boat of Ra. Chapters LXVIII to LXX gave it complete freedom of movement in heaven and on earth.

Chapter LXXI is a series of speeches to the Seven Spirits who punished the wicked in the Realm of Osiris, and Chapter LXXII helped the deceased be reborn in the Mesqet Chamber. The Mesqet was originally the skin of a bull in which the deceased was wrapped. Chapter LXXIII is the same as Chapter IX. Chapters LXXIV and LXXV ensured a passage for the deceased in the Boat Hennu of Sokar, the god of death, and chapter LXXVI brought to its aid the praying mantis that guided it through the "bush" to the House of Osiris. By the recitation of Chapters LXXVII and LXXX-VIII, that is, the "Chapters of Transformations," the deceased was enabled to assume at will the forms of (1) the Golden Falcon, (2) the Divine Falcon, (3) the Great Self-Created God, (4) the god of light or the mantle of Nu, (5) the pure lily, (6) the son of Ptah, (7) the bird Bennu, (8) the heron, (9) the soul of Ra, (10) the Swallow, (11) Sata or Earth Serpent, (12) and the Crocodile. Chapter LXXX-IX brought the soul (ba) of the deceased to its body in the Tuat, and Chapter XC preserved it from mutilations and attacks from the god who "cut off heads and cut off foreheads." Chapters XCI and XCII prevented the soul of the deceased from being enclosed in the tomb. Chapter XCIII is a very difficult spell to understand. Chapters XCIV and XCV provided the deceased with the books of

Vignette from the *Book of the Dead* of the Egyptian adviser Yuya.

Thoth and the power of this god, and allowed it to take his place as Osiris' scribe. Chapters XCVI and XCVII also place it under the protection of Thoth. The narration of Chapter XCVIII provided the deceased with a boat to sail through the northern skies and a ladder to ascend to heaven. Chapters XCIX to CIII gave it the use of the magic boat, the mystical name of each part it was obliged to know, and helped it to enter Ra's boat and be with Hathor. Bebait, or praying mantis, took it to the great gods (Chapter CIV), and the Udjat amulet from Ra's neck provided its double (ka) and its soul-heart (ba) with offerings (Chapters CV, CVI). Chapters CVII to CIX made it favorably known to the spirits of East and West, and to the gods of the Mountain of Sunrise. In this region lived the terrible Serpent-God Ami-hem-f; it was 30 cubits (50 feet) long. In the East, the deceased saw the Morning Star and the Two Sycamores, among which the Sun-God appeared daily, and found the entrance to Sekhet-Aaru or Elysian Fields. Chapter CX and its vignette of the Elysian Fields were already described. Chapters CXI and CXII describe how Horus temporarily lost sight of his eye when looking at Set in the form of a black pig, and chapter CXIII refers to the legend of Horus' drowning and the recovery of his body by Sobek, the crocodile god. Chapter CXIV allowed the deceased to absorb the wisdom of Thoth and his Eight gods. Chapters CXV to CXXII made it master of the Tuats of Memphis and Heliopolis, and provided it with food, and chapter CXXIII allowed it to identify with Thoth. Chapters CXXIV and CXXV, which deal with the Sentence, were already described. Chapter CXXVI contains a prayer to the Four Sacred Monkeys, chapter CXXVII a hymn to the gods of the "Circles" in the Tuat, and chapter CXX-VIII a hymn to Osiris. Chapters CXXX and CXXXI ensured the deceased the use of the Sunrise and Sunset Boats, and Chapter CXXXII allowed it to return to Earth and visit the house in which it had lived. Chapter CXXXVII describes a series of magical ceremonies that were to be performed daily for the deceased in order to make it a "living soul forever." It is said that the formulas were composed during the fourth dynasty. Chapter CXXXVIII refers to the ceremony of reconstitution of Osiris, and chapters CXL-CXLII deal with the creation of twelve altars and the making of offerings to all the gods and the several forms of Osiris. Chapter CXLIII consists of a series of vignettes; three of them depict solar boats.

Chapters CXLIV and CXLVII deal with the Seven Great Halls (Arit) of the Realm of Osiris. The gate of each Hall was guarded by a gatekeeper, a watchman, and a messenger; the first one guarded the door, the second one took care of the arrival of visitors, and the third one took their names to Osiris. No one could enter a Hall without repeating its name, and the names of the gatekeeper, the watchman and the messenger. According to a late tradition, the Gates of the Realm of Osiris were twenty-one (Chapters CXLV and CXLVI), and each had a magical name, and each was guarded by one or two gods, whose names had to be repeated by the deceased before it could pass. Chapter CXLVIII provided the deceased with the names of the Seven Cows and their Bull, on which the "gods" were supposed to feed. Chapters CXLIX and CL give the names of the Fourteen Aats, or districts, of the Realm of Osiris. Chapters *CLI-A and *CLI-B present an image of the mummy chamber and the magical texts necessary to protect the chamber and the mummy contained within. Chapter CLII provided a home for the deceased in Heavenly Anu, and Chapters *CLIII-A and *CLIII-B allowed its soul to avoid capture in the net of the lassoer of souls. Chapter CLIV is a speech to Osiris in which the deceased says: "I will not decay, I will not rot, I will not become worms, I will not see corruption. I will have my being, I will live, I will flourish, I will resurrect in peace."

Chapters CLV to CLXVII are spells that were engraved on amulets, giving the deceased the protection of Ra, Osiris, Isis, Horus, and other gods. The remaining chapters (CLXVIII to CXC) are of varied character, and few of them are found in more than one or two papyri of the Book of the Dead. Some contain hymns that are not prior to the 18th dynasty, and one is an extract from the text on the Pyramid of Unas (lines 379-399). The most interesting is, maybe, chapter CLXXV, which describes the Tuat as airless, waterless and lightless. In this chapter, the deceased is assured of immortality in the words: "You will live for millions of years, a life of millions of years."

Wallis E. A. Budge.
Department of Egyptian and Assyrian Antiquities, British Museum.
April 15, 1920.

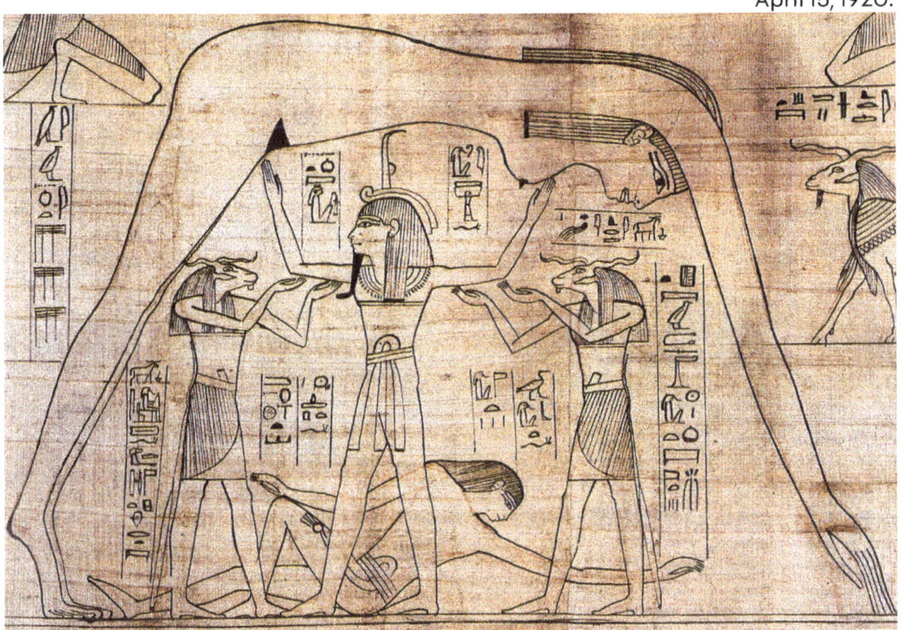

The god Geb and the goddess Nut, in the Greenfield Papyrus

PART II
Hymns

Cat killing a snake in front of the Iched Tree (illustration from chapter 17 of the *Book of the Dead*). Deir el-Medina, 12th–11th centuries BC.

Hymn to Ra

[From the Papyrus of Ani (British Museum N 10470, sheet 20)].

A HYMN OF PRAISE TO RA WHEN HE RISES IN THE EASTERN PART OF HEAVEN. Those who are in your wake rejoice, and here is Osiris Ani, victorious, who says:

"Hail, you Disk, you lord of rays, who rises on the horizon day by day! Shine with your rays of light on the face of Osiris Ani, who is victorious; for at dawn, he sings hymns of praise to you and makes you sit at dusk with words of worship. May the soul of Osiris Ani, the triumphant, come with you to Heaven, may he leave in the boat Matet. May he reach the port in the boat Sektet and may he open his way among the stars that never rest in the Skies."

Osiris Ani, being in peace and in triumph, worships his lord, the lord of eternity, saying: "Homage to you, oh, Herukhuti (Harmachis), who are the god Khepera, the self-created; when you rise on the horizon and shed your rays of light over the lands of the north and south, you are beautiful, yes beautiful, and all the gods rejoice when they behold you, the king of Heaven. The goddess Nebt-Unnut is upon your head, and her southern and northern uræi are on your forehead; she takes her place before you. The god Thoth is in the bow of your boat to completely destroy all your enemies. Those who are in the Tuat (underworld) come to meet you, and bow in homage as they come towards you, to behold [your] beautiful image. And I came before you so that I could be with you to behold your Disk every day. May I not be shut up [in the tomb], may I not turn back, may the limbs of my body be renewed again when I see your beauties, as [are those of] all your favored ones, because I am one of those who worshiped you [while I lived] on Earth. May I enter the Land of Eternity, may I go to the Land of Eternity, for behold, oh my lord, this you commanded me."

And here is Osiris Ani, triumphant in peace, glorious, who says: "Homage to you, oh, you who rise on the horizon as Ra, you rest upon the law [which does not change nor can be altered]. You pass

The Book of the Dead of Hunefer, folio 3.

over the sky, and all faces watch you and your course, for you have been hidden from their gaze. You show yourself at dawn and dusk, day after day. The boat Sektet, where your majesty is, sets sail with vigor; your rays [shine] upon [all] faces; [the number] of your red and yellow rays cannot be known, nor can your bright rays be counted. The Lands of the Gods and the Land of Punt must be seen before what is hidden [in you] can be measured. Alone and by yourself, you manifest yourself [when] you come into existence above Nu (the Sky). May Ani go forward, just as you go forward; may he never stop [moving forward], just as Your Majesty never stops [moving forward], even if it is for a moment, because with large steps you pass in a small moment through spaces that would need hundreds of thousands and millions of years [for man to pass; this] you do, and then go down to rest. You put an end to the hours of the night and you yourself count them; you finish them in the period you designate, and the Earth becomes light. You place yourself before your work in the likeness of Ra; you rise on the horizon."

Osiris, the scribe Ani, triumphant, declares his praise to you when you shine, and when you rise at dawn, he shouts with joy at your birth: "You are crowned with the majesty of your beauties; you shape your limbs as you go forward and bring them without labor pains into the form of Ra, as you rise to the upper air. Grant that I may go to Heaven, which is eternal, and to the mountain where your loved ones live. May I join those bright, holy, and perfect beings who are in the underworld, and may I come with them to behold your beauties when you shine in the evening and go to your mother Nu. You set in the west, and my two hands [raise] in worship [to you] when you set as a living being. Behold, you are the creator of eternity and you are worshiped [when] you set yourself in the Skies. I gave you my heart without wavering, oh you who are more powerful than the gods."

Osiris Ani, triumphant, said: "A hymn of praise to you, oh you who rise like gold, and who flood the world with light on the day of your birth. Your mother gives birth to you in [her] hand, and you give birth to the course of the disk. Oh, you great light, who shine in the Skies, you strengthen the generations of men with the flooding of the Nile and cause joy in all lands, in all cities and in all temples. You are glorious because of your splendors, and you strengthen your ka (double) with hu and tchefau foods. Oh, you who are the mighty one of victories, you who are the power of [all] powers, who strengthen your throne against evil demons, who are glorious in majesty in the boat Sektet, who are extremely mighty in the boat Matet, make Osiris Ani glorious, with victory in the underworld; grant that in the underworld he may be without evil. I pray you to lay aside [his] faults: grant that he may be one of your venerable servants who are with the resplendent ones, that he may

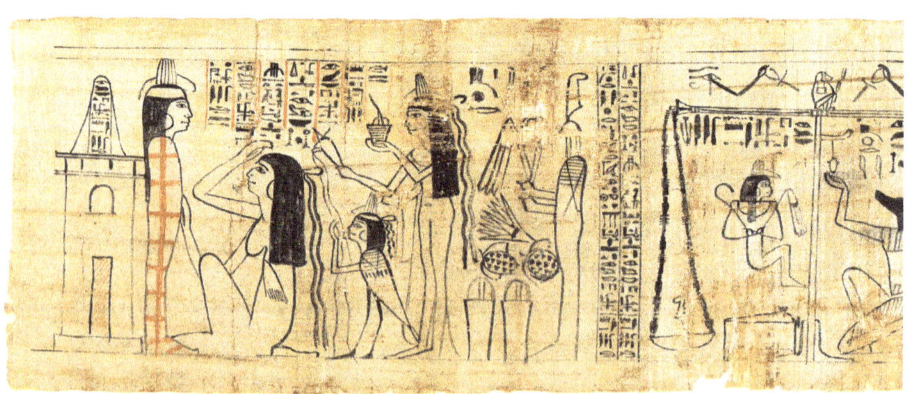

Detail from the Book of the Dead of the singer Tiye.

unite with the souls that are in Ta-tchesertet, and that he may travel to Sekhet-Aaru by a prosperous and happy decree, he, Osiris the scribe Ani, triumphant."

And the god said:

"You will go to Heaven, you will pass through the Sky, you will be reunited with the starry deities. Praises will be offered to you in your boat, you will be praised in the boat Matet, you will see Ra in his sanctuary, you will be together with his disk day by day, you will see the Ant fish when it appears in the turquoise waters, and you will see the Abtu fish in its time. It will happen that the Evil One will fall when he sets a snare to destroy you, and the joints of his neck and of his back will be cut into pieces. Ra [sails] with a fair wind, and the boat Sektet goes forward and arrives at the port. The sailors of Ra rejoice, and the heart of Nebt-ankh is happy, for her lord's enemy fell. You will see Horus in the place of the pilot of the boat, and Thoth and Maat standing each on one of his sides. All the gods will rejoice when they see Ra coming in peace to make the hearts of those who shine live, and Osiris Ani, victorious, the scribe of the divine offerings of the lords of Thebes, will be with them!"

Driving Back Rerek

[From the Papyrus of Mes-em-neter (see Naville, op. cit., Bd. I. Bl. 53)].

THE CHAPTER OF DRIVING THE SERPENT REREK BACK TO THE UNDERWORLD.

Osiris Mes-em-neter said:

"Get back, depart, withdraw from [me], oh Apep, withdraw, or you will be drowned in the Lake of Nu, in the place where your father ordered your slaughter to be carried out. Get away from the divine birthplace of Ra where your terror is. I am Ra who dwells in his terror. Return, demon, before the darts of his rays. Ra overthrew your words, the gods turned your face backwards, the lynx tore your chest, the scorpion fixed fetters on you and Maat sent your destruction. Those who stand in the way knocked you down. Fall down and depart, oh Apep, enemy of Ra! Oh, you who pass over the eastern part of heaven with the sound of the roaring thunder-cloud; oh, Ra, who opens the gates of the horizon immediately on your appearance, [Apep] fell helpless under [your] blows. I accomplished your will, oh Ra, I accomplished your will. I did what is fair; I did what is fair, I worked for the peace of Ra. [I] made to advance your fetters, oh, Ra, and Apep fell through your strong blows. The gods of the south and the north, of the west and the east, fastened chains upon him, and immobilized him with fetters. The god Rekes knocked him down, and the god Hertit chained him. Ra defines, Ra defines. Ra is strong in what he defines. Apep fell, Apep, the enemy of Ra, departs. Greater is the punishment [that was inflicted on you] than the sting that is in the Scorpion goddess, and she, whose course is eternal, powerfully worked on you and with deadly effect. You will never enjoy the delights of love, you will never fulfill your desire, oh Apep, you enemy of Ra! He makes you return, oh, you who are hateful to Ra. He looks at you. Get back! [He] pierces [your] head, [he] cuts off your face, [he] splits [your] head on both sides of the paths, and it is crushed in his land. Your bones are torn to pieces, your limbs are ripped off from you, and the god [A]ker condemned you, oh, Apep, you enemy of Ra! Your sailors are those who keep the reckoning for you, [oh, Ra, as you] go forward, and you rest there, where offerings are made to you [as you] go forward, [as you] go forward to the House, the advance you make towards the Chamber is a prosperous advance. Let no evil obstacle come out of your mouth against me when you work in my favor. I am Set who released the storm clouds and the thunder on the horizon, just as [does] the god Netcheb-ab-f."

"'Hail,' says the god Tem, 'strengthen your faces, oh soldiers of Ra, for I repelled the god Nentcha in the presence of the divine sovereign princes.' 'Hail,' says the god Geb, 'make firm those who are in their seats in the boat of Khepera, let them take their ways, [bringing] their weapons of war in their hands.' 'Hail,' says Hathor, 'take your armor.' 'Hail,' says Nut, 'come and reject the god Tcha who persecutes the one who dwells in his sanctuary and who goes his way alone, that is, Neb-er-tcher, who cannot be repelled'.

'Hail', say those gods who dwell in their company and who surround the Turquoise lagoon, 'come, oh Mighty One, we praise and we will deliver the Mighty One [who dwells in] the divine Sanctuary, from whom proceeds the company of the gods, may celebrations be made for him, may praise be given to him, may words [of praise] be recited before him by you and by me.' 'Hail,' says Nut to the one who is dear to her. 'Hail,' say those who dwell among the gods, 'he comes, he finds [his] way, he makes captives among the gods, he took possession of the goddess Nut, and Geb stands up.' The company of the gods is on the march. Hathor trembles with terror, and Ra triumphs over Apep."

Chapter About the Victory Over Enemies

[From the Papyrus of Nebseni (British Museum N 9900, sheet 12)].

"Hail, Thoth, who made Osiris triumph over his enemies, snare the enemies of Osiris, the scribe Nebseni, the lord of piety, in the presence of the great sovereign princes of all the gods and all the goddesses; in the presence of the great sovereign princes who are in Anu (Heliopolis) on the night of the battle and the overthrow of the demon Sebau in Tattu; on the night of raising double Tet in Sekhem (Letopolis); on the night of night things in Sekhem, in Pe and in Tepu; on the night of the establishment of Horus in the inheritance of his father's things in the double land of Rekhti; on the night that Isis mourns next to her brother Osiris in Abtu (Abydos); on the night of the Haker festival of the distinction [between] the dead (i.e., the damned) and the khus in the path of the dead (i.e., the damned); on the night of judgment of those who will be annihilated in the great [festival of] plowing and turning the earth in Naare-rut-f in Re-stau, and on the night of making Horus triumph over his enemies. Horus is powerful, the northern band southern halves of Heaven rejoice, Osiris is pleased with this and his heart is happy. Hail, Thoth, make Osiris triumph, the scribe Nebseni, over his enemies in the presence of the sovereign princes of all the gods and all the goddesses, and in your presence, sovereign princes who judged Osiris in the sanctuary."

Opening the Mouth of Osiris

[From the Papyrus of Ani (British Museum N 10470, sheet 15)]

THE CHAPTER OF OPENING THE MOUTH OF OSIRIS. The scribe Ani, triumphant, said:

"May the good Ptah open my mouth, and may the god of my city loose the bandages, even the bandages that are over my mouth. Furthermore, may Thoth, being full and equipped with spells, come and loose the bandages, even the bandages of Set that bind my mouth, and may the god Tem throw them at those who chained me with them and drove them away. May my mouth be opened. May my mouth be opened by Shu with his iron knife, with which he opened the mouths of the gods. I am the goddess Sekhet, and I sit in [my] place in the great wind of Heaven. I am the great goddess Sah who dwells among the Souls of Anu (Heliopolis). Now as for all the spells and all the words that can be said against me, may the gods resist them, and may everyone in the company of the gods resist them."

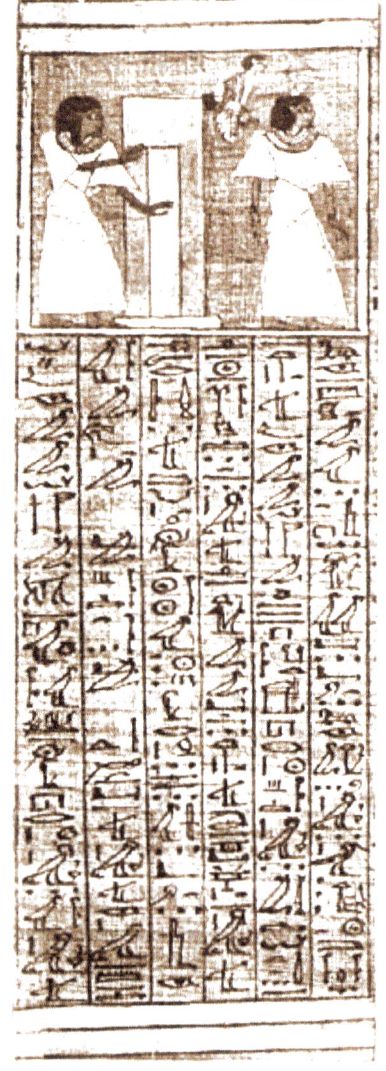

Vignette and text from the Theban Book of the Dead from the Papyrus of Ani [Brit. Mus., N 10470], 18th dynasty.

The judgment of the soul (detail).

Preserving the Heart I

[From the Papyrus of Ani (British Museum N 10470, sheet 15)].

THE CHAPTER OF NOT LETTING THE HEART OF OSIRIS, THE SCRIBE OF THE HOLY OFFERINGS OF ALL THE GODS, ANI, TRIUMPHANT, BE TAKEN AWAY FROM HIM IN THE UNDERWORLD. He says:

"My heart, my mother; my heart, my mother! My heart for which I came to be! May nothing be able to oppose me in [my] judgment. May there be no opposition to me in the presence of the sovereign princes (Tchatcha). May there be no separation between you and me in the presence of the one who keeps the balance! You are my ka, the inhabitant of my body. The god Khmunu who interweaves and strengthens my limbs. May you come to the place of happiness where we are going. May the Shenit[2], which form the conditions of men's lives, not make my name stink. [May it be satisfactory for us, and may listening be satisfactory for us, and may there be joy of heart for us when words are weighing. Let not falsehood be pronounced against me before the great god, the Lord of Amentet. Truly how great you will be when you rise in triumph]!"[3]

---

2 The divine officials of the court of Osiris.

3 The words in brackets are translated from the Papyrus of Nebseni (sheet 4).

Preserving the Heart II

[From Lepsius, "Todtenbuch," Bl. 16].

THE CHAPTER OF NOT LETTING THE HEART OF A MAN BE TAKEN AWAY FROM HIM IN THE UNDERWORLD. Osiris Auf-ankh, victorious, born of Sheret-Amsu, triumphant, said:

"My heart, my mother; my heart, my mother! My heart of my existence on earth. Nothing can oppose me in my judgment. May there be no opposition to me in the presence of sovereign princes. May [no evil] be done against me in the presence of the gods. May there be no separation [from you and] from me in the presence of the great god, the Lord of Amentet. Homage to you, oh heart of Osiris-khent-Amentet! Homage to you, oh my reins! Homage to you, oh gods who dwell in the divine clouds, and who are exalted (or holy) because of your scepters! Speak fair words to Osiris Auf-ankh, and make him prosper before Nehebka. And behold, although I am united with the Earth, and I am in the mightiest part of Heaven, let me remain on the Earth and not die in Amentet, and let me be a khu therein forever and ever."

THIS [CHAPTER] MUST BE RECITED OVER A BASALT SCARAB BEETLE, WHICH WILL BE PLACED IN A GOLDEN FRAME, AND PLACED INSIDE THE HEART OF THE MAN FOR WHOM THE CEREMONIES OF "OPENING THE MOUTH" AND OF ANOINTING WITH OINTMENT WERE PERFORMED. AND THE WORDS WILL BE RECITED AS A MAGIC SPELL: "MY HEART, MY MOTHER; MY HEART, MY MOTHER! MY HEART OF TRANSFORMATIONS."

Preserving the Heart III

[From the Papyrus of Nu (British Museum N 10477, sheet 5)]

THE CHAPTER OF NOT LETTING THE HEART OF THE SUPER-INTENDENT OF THE PALACE, THE CHANCELLOR-IN-CHIEF, NU, TRIUMPHANT, BE TAKEN AWAY FROM HIM IN THE UN-DERWORLD. He said:

"Oh, my heart, my mother! Oh, my heart, my mother! Oh, heart of my existence on Earth. May nothing be able to oppose me in the judgment in the presence of the lords who will judge me. Let it not be said of me and what I did: 'He did acts against what is right and true.' Nothing can be said against me in the presence of the great god, the lord of Amentet. Homage to you, oh, my heart! Homage to you, oh, my heart! Homage to you, oh, my reins! Homage to you, oh, gods who dwell in the divine clouds and who are exalted (or holy) because of your scepters! Speak [for me] fair things to Ra and make me prosper before Nehebka. And behold me, even though I am united with the Earth in its mighty innermost parts, let me remain on the Earth and not let me die in Amentet, but become a khu therein."

Vignette and Chapter of the *Book of the Dead* written in hieratic for Heru-em-Heb [Brit. Mus., N 10257] 26th dynasty, or later.

Opening the Underworld

[From the Papyrus of Nu (British Museum N 10477, sheet 15)].

THE CHAPTER OF OPENING THE UNDERWORLD. The superintendent of the palace, the chancellor-in-chief, Nu, triumphant, says:

"The chamber of those who dwell in Nu is opened, and the steps of those who dwell with the god of Light are freed. The chamber of Shu is opened, and he goes out; and I will go out, and I will advance from my territory (...), I will receive... and I will hold firmly to the tribute in the House of the Chief of his dead. I will advance to my throne, which is in the boat of Ra. I will not be molested, and I will

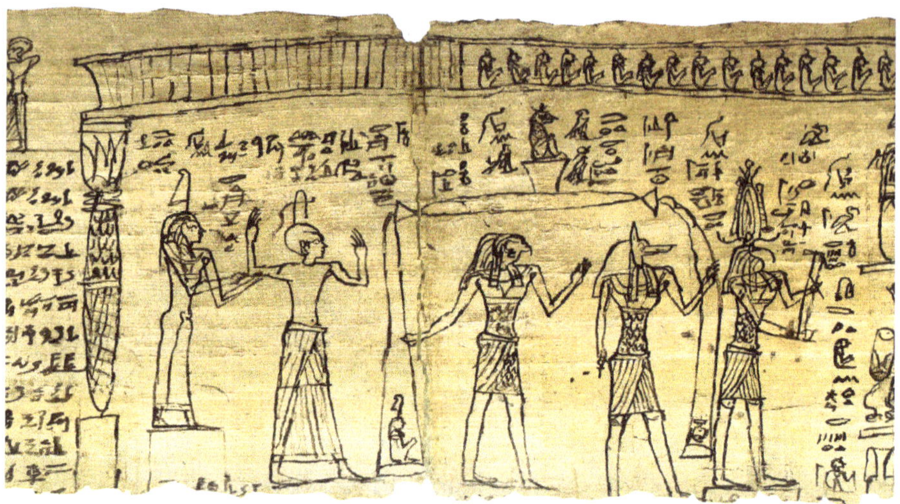

The Funerary Book of Peteminis, 2nd century BC.

not suffer shipwreck from my throne, which is in the boat of Ra, the mighty one. Hail the one who shines and gives light from Hent-she!"

Coming Forth by Day

[From the Papyrus of Nu (British Museum N 10477, sheet 7)].

THE CHAPTER OF COMING FORTH BY DAY. The superintendent of the palace, the chancellor-in-chief, Nu, triumphant, says:

"The doors of heaven are open to me; the doors of earth are open to me; the bars and bolts of Geb are open to me; and the first temple was untied for me by the god Petra. Behold, I was guarded and watched, [but now] I am free; behold, his hand had tied ropes about me, and his hand had tied itself over me on earth. Re-hent was open to me and Re-hent was untied before me, Re-hent was given to me, and I will come forth by day to any place I want. I gained the mastery over my heart; I gained the mastery over my chest; I gained the mastery over my two hands; I gained the mastery over my two feet; I gained the mastery over my mouth; I gained the mastery over my entire body; I gained the mastery over the sepulchral offerings; I gained the mastery over the waters; I gained the mastery over the air; I gained the mastery over the canal; I gained the mastery over the river and the land; I gained the mastery over the grooves; I gained the mastery over the men who work for me; I gained the mastery over the women who work for me in the underworld; I gained the mastery over [all] things that were commanded to be done for me on earth, according to the request that you spoke for me [saying]: 'Behold, let him live upon the bread of Geb.' What is an abomination to me, I will not eat; I [will not] live on cakes [made] of white grain, and my beer will be [made] of the red grain of Hapi (that is, the Nile). In a clean place, I will sit on the ground under the date foliage of the goddess Hathor, who dwells in the spacious Disk as it advances towards Anu (Heliopolis), having the books of divine words from the writings of the god Thoth. I gained the mastery over my heart; I gained the mastery over the place (or chest) of my heart; I gained the mastery over my mouth; I gained the mastery over my two hands; I gained the mastery over the waters; I gained the mastery over the canal; I gained the mastery over the river; I gained the mastery over the grooves; I gained the mastery over the men who work for me; I gained the mastery over the women

The Book of the Dead of Pajuheru, Ptolemaic Period, 3rd to 2nd centuries BC.

who work for me in the underworld; I gained the mastery over [all] things that were commanded to be done for me on earth and in the underworld. I will rise up on my left side, and I will stand on my right side; I will stand up on my right side, and I will stand [on my left side]. I will sit down, I will stand up, and I will stand in [the path of] the wind like a well-prepared guide."

IF THIS COMPOSITION IS KNOWN [BY THE DECEASED], IT WILL COME FORTH BY DAY, AND IT WILL BE IN CONDITION TO TRAVEL ON THE EARTH AMONG THE LIVING. AND IT WILL NEVER SUFFER DECREASE, NEVER, NEVER, NEVER.

Of Being Close to Thoth I

[From the Papyrus of Nu (British Museum N 10477, sheet 7)].

THE CHAPTER OF BEING CLOSE TO THOTH. The chancellor-in-chief, Nu, triumphant, said:

"I am the one who sends terror to the powers of rain and thunder and I ward off from the great divine lady the attacks of violence. [I hurt like the god Shat (i.e., the god of slaughter), poured libations of cold water like the god Ashu, and worked for the great divine lady [to ward off] the attacks of violence]. I made [my] knife flourish together with the knife that is in the hand of Thoth in the powers of rain and thunder."

Of Being Close to Thoth II

[From the Papyrus of Nu (British Museum N 10477, sheets 19 and 20)].

THE CHAPTER OF BEING CLOSE TO THOTH AND GIVING GLORY TO A MAN IN THE UNDERWORLD. The chancellor-in-chief, Nu, triumphant, said:

"I am the god Her-ab-maat-f (that is, 'the one who is within his eyes'), and I came to give right and truth to Ra; I made Suti to be in peace with me through offerings made to the god Aker and the Tesheru deities, and [by making] reverence to Geb."

Coming forth by day of the Ba and the shadow of Neferoubenef outside the tomb
(papyrus from the Louvre Museum).

"[The following] words should be recited in the boat Sektet: [Hail,] scepter of Anubis, I made the four khus who are in the wake of the lord of the universe to be in peace with me, and I am the lord of the fields through their decree. I am the divine father Bah (that is, the god of flood), and I quench the thirst of the one who keeps the lakes. Behold me, then, oh, great gods of majesty who dwell among the Souls of Anu, for I am lifted up over you. I am the god Menkh (that is, Gracious) who dwells among you. In truth, I cleaned my soul, oh, great god of majesty, do not put before me the evil obstacles that come out of your mouth, and do not allow destruction to come around me or upon me. I purified myself in the Lake of making one to be in peace, [and in the Lake of] weighing in the scales, and I bathed in Netert-ut-chat, which is under the holy sycamore tree of heaven. Behold, [I am] bathed, [and] I triumphed [over] all [my enemies] that immediately arise and rise up against right and truth. I am right and true on earth. I, myself, spoke with my mouth, [which is] the power of the Lord, the

Only One, Ra the mighty, who lives by right and truth. Let not injury be inflicted upon me, [but let me be] clothed in the day of those who go forward to all [good] things."

Of Transformation into a Falcon

[From the Papyrus of (British Museum N 10.477, sheets 13 and 14).]

THE CHAPTER OF MAKING THE TRANSFORMATION INTO A DIVINE FALCON. The chancellor-in-chief, Nu, triumphant, said:

"Hail, Great God, come now to Tattu! Make my paths plain and let me go around [to visit] my thrones; I renewed myself and raised myself. Oh, grant that I may be feared, and make me a terror. May the gods of the underworld be afraid of me, and may they fight for me in their dwellings that are in it. Let the one who would harm me not come near me or hurt me in the House of Darkness, that is, the one who clothes and covers the weak one, and whose [name] is hidden; and may the gods not act in the same way with me. [Hail], oh gods, who hear [my] speech! Hail, oh rulers, who are among the followers of Osiris! Be silent therefore, oh, gods, when one god speaks to another, for he listens to justice and truth; and what I speak to [him] also speak through me then, oh, Osiris. Grant that I may travel around [according to] what comes out of your mouth concerning me, and grant that I may see your own Form (or forms), and the dispositions of your Souls. May you grant that I come forth, and that I may have power over my legs, and that I may have my existence there like that of Neb-er-tcher who is over [everything]. May the gods of the underworld fear me and fight for me in their dwellings. May you grant that I move along with the divine beings who move on, and may I be established in my resting place as the Lord of Life. May I join Isis, the divine lady, and may she protect me from the one who would harm me; and let no one come and see the divine naked and defenseless. May I travel, may I reach the ends of heaven. I exchange words with the god Geb, I make supplications for the divine food of Neb-er-tcher; the gods of the underworld are afraid of me, and fight for me in their dwellings when they see that you provided me with food, both from the birds of the air and the fish of the sea. I am one of those khus who dwell with the divine khu, and I made my form similar to its divine Form, when it arises and manifests in Tattu. [I am] a spiritual body (sahu) and I possess my soul, and I will speak to you the things that concern me. Oh, grant that I may be feared, and make me a terror; may the gods of the underworld be afraid of me, and may they fight for me in their dwellings. I am the khu who dwells with the divine khu, who the god Tem created, and who arose from the flower (that is, the eyelashes) of his eye; he caused to exist, and he caused to be glorious (that is, to be khu), and he made powerful thereby those who have their existence together with him. See, he is the only one in Nu, and they sing praises (or pay homage) to him [when] he leaves the horizon, and the gods and the khus who came into existence with him attribute [the mastery of] terror to him."

"I am one of those worms that the eye of the Lord, the Only One, created. And behold, when Isis had not yet given birth to Horus, I had germinated, and blossomed, and grew old, and became greater than those who dwelt with the divine khu, and who had arisen along with him. And I arose like the divine falcon, and Horus made for me a spiritual body containing his own soul, so that I might take

The harpooning of Apep.

possession of all that belonged to Osiris in the underworld. The double Lion-God, the ruler of things belonging to the Temple of the crown of Nemes, who dwells in his secret abode, says [to me]: 'Return to the ends of heaven, for behold, since through your form of Horus you became a spiritual body, (sahu) the crown of Nemes is not for you; but behold, you have the power of speech to the ends of heaven.' And I, the guardian, took possession of the things of Horus [that belonged] to Osiris in the underworld, and Horus told me aloud the things that his divine father Osiris spoke to him in [past] years on the day of his own burial. I gave you the crown of Nemes through the double Lion-God so that you may move on and may reach the heavenly path, and that those who dwell in the most distant parts of the horizon may see you, and that the gods of the underworld may see you and can fight for you in their dwellings. And theirs is Auhet. The gods, each and every one of them, who are the guardians of the sanctuary of the Lord, the Only One, fell before my words. Hail! The one who is exalted in his tomb is on my side, and he tied [on my head] the crown of Nemes, by the decree of the double Lion-God in my name, and the god Auhet prepared a way for me. I, myself, I am exalted in my tomb, and the double Lion-God

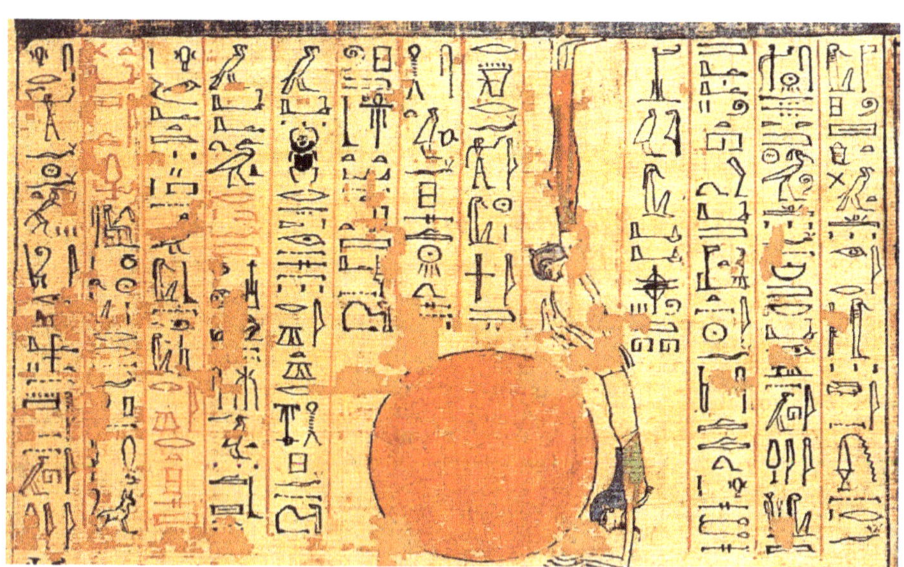

Nun making the Sun rise (detail).

tied the crown of Nemes on my [head], and he also gave me the double hairy covering of my head. He established my heart through his own backbone, he established my heart through his great and extraordinary strength, and I will not go down for Shu. I make peace with the beautiful and divine Brother, the lord of the two uræi, may he be worshiped! I, myself, I am the one who knows the roads through the sky, and their wind is in my body. The bull that casts terror [on men] will not make me retreat, and I will pass over to the place where the castaway lies on the border of the Sekhet- neheh (that is, Field of Unlimited Time), and I will travel into the night and sorrow of the regions of Amenti. Oh, Osiris, I will go every day to the House of the double Lion-God, and I will go from there to the House of Isis, the divine lady. I will contemplate the sacred things that are hidden, and I will be led to the secret and sacred things, as well as I was granted to see the birth of the Great God. Horus made me a spiritual body through his soul, [and I] see what is in him. If I speak near the powerful ones of Shu, they reject my opportunity. I am the guardian and I take possession of the things that Horus had from Osiris in the underworld. I, myself, I am Horus who dwells in the divine khu. [I] gained power over his crown, gained power over his splendor, and traveled through the remote and unlimited parts of heaven. Horus is on his throne; Horus is on his royal throne. My face is like that of the divine falcon, my strength is like that of the divine falcon, and I am someone who was fully equipped by my divine Lord. I will go to Tattu, I will see Osiris, I will pay homage to him on the right and on the left, I will pay homage to Nut, and she will look at me, and the gods will look at me, together with the Eye of Horus that is sightless. They (that is, the gods) will make their arms come to me. I arise [as] a divine power, and [I] reject the one who would subject me to restraint. They open the sacred paths to me, see my form, and hear what I say. [Down] upon your faces, oh, gods of the Tuat (underworld), who would resist me with your faces and oppose me with your powers, who lead along the stars that never rest, and who make the sacred paths to the abode Hemati [where is] the Lord of the extremely powerful and terrible Soul.

Horus ordered you to lift your faces so that I could look at you. I arose like the divine falcon, and Horus made me a spiritual body, through his own soul, to take possession of what belongs to Osiris in the Tuat (underworld). I bound the gods with divine braids and traveled to those who guard their quarters and who were on both sides of me. I made my roads and traveled, and reached those divine beings who dwell in their secret abodes and who are guardians of the Temple of Osiris. I spoke to them with strength, and made them know the mightier power of the one who is provided with two horns [to fight] against Suti; and I made them know about the one who took possession of the divine food, and who is provided with the Power of Tem. May the gods of the underworld [command] a prosperous journey for me! Oh, gods who dwell in your secret abodes, and who are guardians of the Temple of Osiris, and whose numbers are great and numerous, grant that I may come to you. I connected and gathered the powers of Kesemu-enenet, or (as others say), Kesemiu-enenet; and I sanctified the Powers of the paths of those who watch over and protect the roads of the horizon, and who are the guardians of the horizon of Hemati which is in the sky. I established dwellings for Osiris, I made the paths sacred to him, I did what was commanded, I came to Tattu, I saw Osiris, I spoke to him about the affairs of his firstborn son, whom he loves, and about the wound in Suti's heart, and I saw the divine, who is lifeless. Yes, I made them know about the councils of the gods that Horus carried out while his father, Osiris, was not [with him]. Hail, Lord, powerful and terrible soul! In truth I, myself, came; look at me and make me exalted. I made my way through the Tuat (underworld), and opened the paths that belong to heaven and also those that belong to earth, and I was not opposed to them. Exalted [be you] on your throne, oh, Osiris! You heard beautiful things, oh, Osiris! Your strength is vigorous, oh, Osiris. Your head is attached to you, oh, Osiris. Your forehead is established, oh, Osiris. Your heart is happy, [oh, Osiris]. Your speech is established, [oh, Osiris], and your princes rejoice. You are established as the Bull of Amentet. Your son Horus was born like the Sun on your throne, and all life is with him. Millions of years minister to him, and millions of years frighten him; the company of the gods are his servants, and the company of the gods fear him. The god Tem, the Governor and only one of the gods, spoke [these things], and his word does not pass away. Horus is both divine food and sacrifice. [He] passed to gather [the limbs of] his divine father; Horus is [his] liberator, Horus is [his] liberator. Horus arose from the water of his divine father and [from his] decay. He became the governor of Egypt. The gods worked for him and worked for him for millions of years; and he caused to live millions of years through his Eye, the Only One of his Lord (or Neb-s), Nebt-er- tcher."

Chapter of Bringing Charms to Osiris

[From the Papyrus of Ani (British Museum N 10470, sheet 15)].

THE CHAPTER OF BRINGING CHARMS TO OSIRIS ANI [IN THE UNDERWORLD]. He says:

"I am Tem-Khepera, who was created on the thigh of his divine mother. Those who are in Nu (i.e., the sky) are like wolves, and those who are among the sovereign princes become hyenas. Behold, I gather the charm [of every place where] it is, and of every man it is with, faster than greyhounds and faster than light. Hail, you who tow along the boat Makhent of Ra, the props of your sails and your rudder are stretched to the wind as you sail to the Lake of Fire in the underworld. Behold, you gather the charm of every place where it is, and of every man it is with, faster than greyhounds and faster than light, [the charm] that created the ways of being of... mother, and that or creates the gods or silences them, and which gives the heat of fire to the gods. Behold, charm is given to me, from wherever it is [and whoever it is with], faster than greyhounds and faster than light," or (as others say) "faster than a shadow."

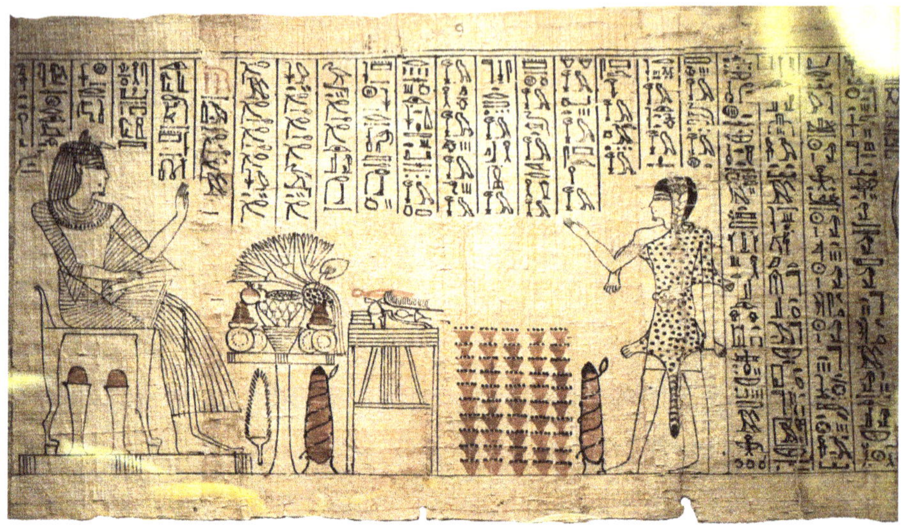

The Funerary Book of the priest of Amun Khonsu-remp.

Chapter of Giving a Heart to Osiris

[From the Papyrus of Ani (British Museum N 10470, sheet 15).]

THE CHAPTER OF GIVING A HEART TO OSIRIS ANI IN THE UNDERWORLD. He says:

"May my heart (ab) be with me in the House of Hearts! May my heart be with me in the House of Hearts! May my heart be with me, and may it rest there, [or] I will not eat of the cakes of Osiris on the eastern side of the Lake of Flowers, neither will I have a boat to go down the Nile, nor another to go up to, nor can I go down the Nile with you. Let my mouth [be given] to me so that I may speak, and my two legs to walk, and my two hands and arms to defeat my enemy. May the doors of heaven be opened to me; may Geb, the Prince of the gods, open wide his two jaws for me; may he open my two eyes that are blindfolded; may he make me stretch my two legs that are tied together; and may Anpu (Anubis) make my thighs firm so that I can stand upon them. May the goddess Sekhet make me rise so that I may ascend to heaven, and may what I command be done in the House of the ka (double) of Ptah (that is, Memphis). I understand with my heart. I gained the mastery over my heart, I gained the mastery over my two hands, I gained mastery over my legs, I gained power to do whatever my ka (double) wants. My soul will not be chained to my body at the gates of the underworld; but I will enter in peace, and I will come forth in peace."

Mastery Over Elements
[From Lepsius, "Todtenbuch," Bl. 23]

ANOTHER CHAPTER. Osiris Auf-ankh, triumphant, said:

"May the gates of heaven be opened for me by the god [Thoth] and by Hapi, and let me pass through the doors of Ta-qebh into the great heaven," or (as others say), "at the moment," [or (as others say)], "with the strength of Ra. Grant, [oh, Thoth and Hapi], that I may have power over water, as well as Set had power over his enemies in the day when there were storms and rain upon the earth. Let me have power over the divine beings who have mighty arms on their shoulders, as the god who is clothed in splendor, and whose name is unknown, had power over them; and may I have power over beings whose arms are powerful."

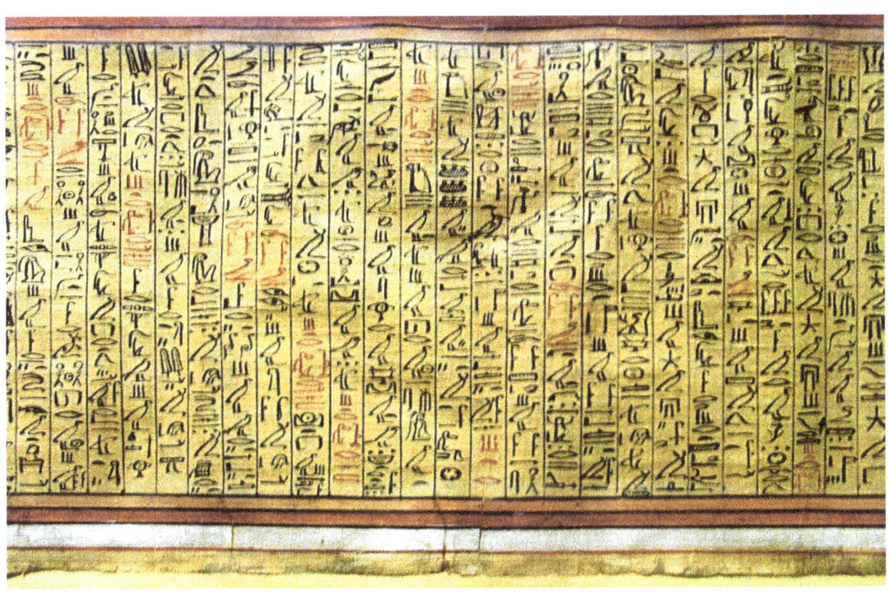

Detail of a funerary book (Museum of Turin, Italy).

Of Sekhet-Hetepet

[From the Papyrus of Nebseni (British Museum N 9900, sheet 17)].

HERE BEGIN THE CHAPTERS OF SEKHET-HETEPET, AND THE CHAPTERS OF COMING FORTH BY DAY; OF ENTERING AND LEAVING THE UNDERWORLD; OF COMING TO SEKHET-AARU; OF BEING IN SEKHET-HETEPET, THE MIGHTY LAND, THE LADY OF THE WINDS; OF HAVING POWER THERE; OF BECOMING A KHU THERE; OF PLOWING THERE; OF HARVESTING THERE; OF EATING THERE; OF DRINKING THERE; OF MAKING LOVE THERE; AND OF DOING EVERYTHING AS A MAN DOES ON EARTH.

Here is the scribe and artist of the Temple of Ptah, Nebseni, who says: "Set took possession of Horus, who looked with both eyes at the building around Sekhet-Hetepet, but I freed Horus [and took him from] Set, and Set opened the paths of both eyes [which are] in heaven. Set cast his moisture to the winds over the soul [that has] his day (or his eye) and that dwells in the city of Mert, and he freed the inside of the body of Horus from the gods of Akert. See me now, for I made this mighty boat to travel upon the Lake of Hetepet, and I brought it in strength from the palace of Shu; the mastery of his stars rejuvenates and renews his former strength. I brought the boat to his lakes so that I could go out to his cities, and I sailed to his divine city, Hetepet. And behold, it is because I, myself, am in peace with his seasons, and with his guidance, and with his territory, and with the company of the gods who are his firstborn. He causes the two divine fighters (that is, Horus and Set) to be in peace with those who watch over the living that he created in a fair way, and he brings peace [with him]; he causes the two divine fighters to be in peace with those who watch over them. He cuts the hair of divine warriors, he drives away the storm from the defenseless, and he keeps evil away from the khus. Let me gain mastery within this field, for I know it, and I sailed among his lakes to enter his cities. My mouth is strong; and I am equipped [with weapons to use] against the khus; let them not have the mastery over me. Let me be rewarded with your fields, oh, you, god of Hetepet; what is your wish, you will do, oh, lord of the winds. May I become a khu therein, may I eat, may I drink, may I wash, may I harvest, may I fight, may I make love, may my words be powerful, may I never be in a state of servitude in it, but that I may be in authority in it. You made strong the mouth and throat of the god of Hetepet; Qetetbu is his name. He is established over the watery supports of the god Shu, and is connected with the pleasant things of Ra. He is the divider of years, he is hidden from the mouth, his mouth is silent, what he utters is secret, he fulfills eternity and takes possession of the eternity of existence as lord of Hetepet. The god Horus becomes strong like the falcon that is a thousand cubits long and two thousand [cubits wide] in life; he has equipment with him, and he travels back and forth wherever his heart wants in his lakes and in his cities. He was begotten in the birth chamber of the city god, he has offerings [made to him] of the food of the city god, he performs what is proper to do there, and the union of this, in the matter of all the birth chambers of the divine city. When [he] establishes life as a crystal, he performs everything in it, and these things are similar to the things that are done in the Lake of Double Fire, where there is no one who rejoices and where there are all kinds of evil things. The god of Hetepet enters and leaves, and retreats [in] the Field that gathers all kinds of things to the birth chamber of the city god. When he establishes life as a crystal, he performs all kinds of things in it that are similar to the things that are done in the Lake of Double Fire, where there is no one who rejoices, and where there are evil things. [Let me] live with the god of Hetepet, clothed and not despoiled by the lords of the north, and may the lords of divine things bring me food; may he bring me forward and may I go forth, and may he bring my power to me there, and may I receive it, and may my equipment be of the god of Hetepet. May I gain mastery over the great and powerful word that is in my body in this place of mine, and by doing so, I will remember and forget. Let me go forward on my journey, and let me plow. I am at peace in the divine city, and I know the waters, cities, nomes, and lakes that are in Sekhet-Hetepet. I exist therein, I am strong therein, I become a khu therein, I eat therein, I sow therein, I plow therein,

I harvest therein, I make love therein, I am in peace with the god of Hetepet. Behold, there I scatter the seed, I sail between your lakes and advance to your cities, oh, divine Hetepet. Behold, my mouth is equipped with my horns [for teeth], grant me an overflowing supply of food over which the kas and khus [live]. I made the judgment of Shu on the one who knows him, so that I may go to his cities, and may sail among his lakes, and walk in Sekhet-Hetepet; and behold, Ra is in the sky, and behold, the god of Hetepet is his double offering. I came to his land, I put on my belt, I came so that the gifts that were about to be given to me might be given, I rejoiced for myself. I clung to my strength, which the god of Hetepet greatly increased for me. Oh, Unen-em-hetepet, I entered you, and my soul follows me, and my divine food is in my two hands, oh, Lady of the two lands, who establishes my word by which I remember and forget; I would live without injury, without any injury [being done] to me, oh, grant me, oh, grant me joy of heart. Make me be at peace, tie my tendons and muscles, and make me receive air. Oh, Un[en]-em-hetepet, Lady of the winds, I entered you and opened (that is, showed) my head. Ra falls asleep, but I am awake, and there is the goddess Hast at the gate of the sky at night. Obstacles were placed before me, but I gathered what he issued. I am in my city. Oh, Nut-urt,

Detail of a funerary book with the goddess Isis and the gods Osiris and Horus.

I entered you and counted my harvest, and I go forward to Uakh. I am the Bull wrapped in turquoise, the lord of the Bull Field, the lord of the divine speech of the goddess Sopdet (Sotis) in her hours. Oh, Uakh, I entered you, I ate my bread, I acquired the mastery over choice pieces of meat from oxen and feathered birds, and the birds of Shu were given to me; I follow the gods and [I follow] the divine kas. Oh, Tchefet, I entered you. I dress myself in clothes, and I dress myself with the garment of Ra; now see, [he is] in the sky, and those who dwell in it follow Ra, and [I] follow Ra in the sky. Oh, Unen-em-hetepet, lord of the two lands, I entered you and dove into the lakes of Tchesert; here I am, for all filth was moved away from me. The Great God grows in it, and behold, I found [food in it]; I trapped the feathered birds and fed on the best [of them]. Oh, Qenqentet, I entered you, and I saw Osiris [my father], and I beheld my mother, and I made love. I caught the worms and the serpents, and I am free. And I know the name of the god who is opposite to the goddess of Tchesert, and who has straight hair and is equipped with two horns; he reaps, and I wash and reap. Oh, Hast, I entered you, drove away those who wanted to come to the turquoise sky, and followed the winds of the company of the gods. The Great God gave my head to me, and the one who tied my head to me is the Mighty One who has turquoise eyes, that is, Ari-en-ab-f (that is, he does what he wants). Oh, Usert, I entered you in the head of the house, where divine food is brought to me. Oh, Smam, I entered you. My heart watches, my head is equipped with the white crown, I am carried to the heavenly regions, and I cause earthly objects to flourish, and there is joy of heart for the Bull, for the heavenly beings, and for the company of the gods. I am the god who is the Bull, the lord of the gods, as he comes out of the turquoise [sky]. Oh, divine nome of wheat and barley, I came to you, I approached you and accepted what follows me, that is, the best of libations from the company of the gods. I tied my boat in the heavenly lakes, raised the pole to anchor, recited the prescribed words with my voice, and assigned praises to the gods who dwell in Sekhet-Hetepet."

Apep being harpooned.

The Chaplet of Victory

[From Lepsius, "Todtenbuch," Bl. 13].

THE CHAPTER OF THE CHAPLET OF VICTORY. Osiris Auf-ankh, victorious, born of Sheret-Amsu, victorious, says:

"Your father Tem wove for you a beautiful crown of victory [to be placed] on [your] living forehead, oh, you who love the gods, and you will live forever. Osiris-khent-Amentet made you triumph over your enemies, and your father Geb decreed for you all his inheritance. Come therefore, oh, Horus, son of Isis, for you, oh, son of Osiris, sit on the throne of your father Ra to defeat your enemies, for he ordered for you the two lands to their extreme limits. Aten [also] ordered this, and the company of the gods confirmed the splendid power of the victory of Horus, son of Isis and son of Osiris, forever and ever. And Osiris Auf-ankh will be victorious forever and ever. Oh, Osiris-khent-Amentet, all the northern and southern parts of heaven, and every god and every goddess that are on earth [will see] the victory of Horus, the son of Isis and the son of Osiris, over his enemies in the presence of Osiris-khent-Amentet who will make Osiris Auf-ankh, victorious, triumph over his enemies in the presence of Osiris-khent-Amentet, Un-nefer, the son of Nut, on the day of making him triumph over Set and his demons in the presence of the great sovereign chiefs who are in Anu (Heliopolis); on the night of the battle and overthrow of the Seba-fiend in the presence of the great sovereign princes who are in Abtu; on the night of making

Osiris triumph over his enemies, make you Osiris Auf-ankh, triumphant, to triumph over his enemies in the presence of the great sovereign princes, who are on the horizon of Amentet; on the day of the festival of Haker in the presence of the great sovereign princes who are in Tattu; on the night of the establishment of Tet in Tattu in the presence of the great sovereign princes who are in the ways of the damned; on the night of the judgment of those who will be annihilated in the presence of the great sovereign princes who are in Sekhem (Letopolis); on the night of the 'things of the altars in Sekhem' in the presence of the great sovereign princes who are in Pe and Tepu; on the night of the establishment of the inheritance by Horus of the things of his father Osiris in the presence of the great sovereign princes who are at the great festival of the plowing and turning up of the earth in Tattu, or (as others say), [in] Abtu; on the night of the weighing of words or (as others say), weighing of locks in the presence of the great sovereign princes who are in An-rut-f in their place; on the night when Horus receives the birth chamber of the gods in the presence of the great sovereign princes who are in the lands of Rekhti; on the night when Isis lies down to watch [and] mourn for her brother in the presence of the great sovereign princes who are in Re-stau; on the night of making Osiris triumph over all his enemies".

Papyrus with instructions about placing amulets.

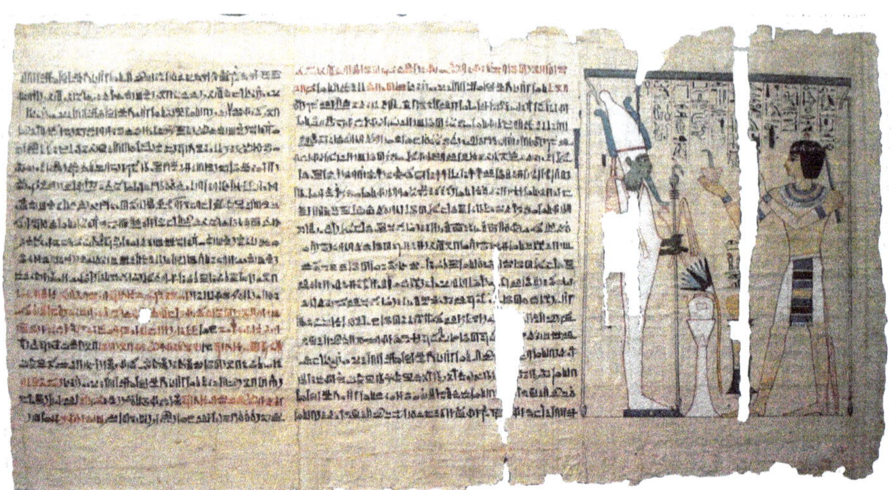

Papyrus of the Book of the Dead of Pinedjem II, 21st dynasty (c. 990–969 BC). The scene depicts Pinedjem II in his role as high priest making an offering to the god Osiris.

Horus repeated [these] words four times, and all his enemies fell on their heads and were thrown down and were cut into pieces; and Osiris Auf-ankh, triumphant, repeated [these] words four times, therefore, let all his enemies fall on their heads, and be thrown down and cut into pieces. Horus, son of Isis and son of Osiris, celebrated successively millions of festivals, and all his enemies fell on their heads, and were thrown down and cut into pieces. Their dwelling has gone forth to the block of the East; their heads were cut off; their necks were destroyed; their thighs were cut off; they were given to the Great Destroyer who dwells in the valley of the grave; and they will never come forth under the restriction of the god Geb.

THIS CHAPTER SHALL BE RECITED OVER THE DIVINE CHAPLET THAT IS PLACED ON THE FACE OF THE DECEASED, AND YOU SHALL THROW INCENSE INTO THE FIRE IN THE NAME OF OSIRIS AUF-ANKH, TRI-UMPHANT, BORN OF SHERET-AMSU, TRIUMPHANT; THUS, YOU WILL MAKE HIM TRIUMPH OVER HIS ENEMIES, DEAD OR ALIVE, AND HE WILL BE AMONG THE FOLLOWERS OF OSIRIS; AND A HAND WILL BE REACHED OUT TO HIM WITH FOOD AND DRINK IN THE PRESENCE OF GOD. [THIS CHAPTER] WILL BE SAID BY YOU TWICE AT DAWN – NOW IT IS A NEVER-FAILING CHARM –, REGULARLY AND CONTINUOUSLY.

Hymn and Litany to Osiris
[From the Papyrus of Ani (British Museum N 10470, sheet 19)].

"Praise be to you, oh, Osiris, lord of eternity, Unnefer, Herukhuti (Harmachis), whose forms are multiple and whose attributes are majestic, Ptah-Seker-Tem in Anu (Heliopolis), the lord of the hidden place, and the creator of Het-ka-Ptah (Memphis) and the gods [therein], the guide of the underworld, whom [the gods] glorify when you establish in Nut. Isis embraces you in peace, and she drives away the demons from the mouth of your paths. You turn your face to Amentet, and make the earth shine like refined copper. Those who lay down (that is, the dead) rise to see you, breathe the air, and look at your face when the Disk appears on the horizon; their hearts are in peace as they behold you, oh, you, who are Eternity and Eternity!"

Litany

"Homage to you, [oh, lord of] the stellar deities in Anu, and of the heavenly beings in Kher-aba; you god Unti, who are more glorious than the gods that are hidden in Anu; oh, grant me a path whereby I may pass in peace, for I am fair and true; I did not intentionally speak lies, I did not do anything deceitfully."

"Homage to you, oh, An-em-Antes, Herukhuti (Harmachis), with long strides you traverse the sky, oh, Heru-khuti. Oh, grant me a path whereby I may pass in peace, for I am fair and true; I did not intentionally speak lies, I did not do anything deceitfully."

"Homage to you, oh, Soul of eternity, you Soul who dwells in Tattu, Unnefer, son of Nut; you are lord of Akert. Oh, grant me a path whereby I may pass in peace, for I am fair and true; I did not intentionally speak lies, I did not do anything deceitfully."

"Homage to you in your dominion over Tattu; the Uraeus crown is established upon your head; you are The One who makes the strength that protects himself, and you dwell in peace in Tattu. Oh, grant me a path whereby I may pass in peace, for I am fair and true; I did not intentionally speak lies, I did not do anything deceitfully."

"Homage to you in your dominion over Tattu; the Uraeus crown is established upon your head; you are The One who makes the strength that protects himself, and you dwell in peace in Tattu. Oh, grant me a path whereby I may pass in peace, for I am fair and true; I did not intentionally speak lies, I did not do anything deceitfully."

"Homage to you, oh, you who are mighty in your hour, you, great and mighty Prince, dweller of An-rut-f, lord of eternity and creator of eternity, you are the lord of Suten-henen (Heracleopolis Magna). Oh, grant me a path whereby I may pass in peace, for I am fair and true; I did not intentionally speak lies, I did not do anything deceitfully."

"Homage to you, oh, you who rest in Right and Truth, you are the lord of Abtu (Abydos), and your limbs are united with Ta-tchesertet; you are the one to whom fraud and cunning are hateful. Oh, grant me a path whereby I may pass in peace, for I am fair and true; I did not intentionally speak lies, I did not do anything deceitfully."

"Homage to you, oh, you who are within your boat, you bring Hapi (that is, the Nile) from its source; the light shines upon your body and you are the dweller of Nekhen. Oh, grant me a path whereby I may pass in peace, for I am fair and true; I did not intentionally speak lies, I did not do anything deceitfully."

"Homage to you, oh, creator of the gods, you King of North and South, oh, Osiris, victorious, ruler of the world in your gracious seasons; you are the lord of the heavenly world. Oh, grant me a path whereby I may pass in peace, for I am fair and true; I did not intentionally speak lies, I did not do anything deceitfully."

Of Bringing the Boat Makhent

[From the Papyrus of Nu (British Museum N 10477, sheets 21 and 22)].

THE CHAPTER OF BRINGING A BOAT IN THE UNDERWORLD. The chancellor-in-chief, Nu, triumphant, said:

"Hail, you who bring the boat over the back of evil [of Apep], grant that I may bring the boat and reel [its] ropes in peace, in peace. Come, come, hurry, hurry, for I have come to see my father Osiris, the lord of the ansi garment, who gained the mastery with joy of heart. Hail, lord of the storm, you Male, you Sailor! Hail, you who sail over the evil back of Apep! Hail, you who bind heads and firm neck bones when you

Detail of the Funerary Book of the high priest Pinedjem II.

emerge from the knives. Hail, you who are in command of the hidden boat, who trap Apep, grant that I bring the boat, and that I may reel the ropes and sail in it. This land is baleful, and the stars became unbalanced and fell upon it, and they found nothing to help them rise again: their path is blocked by the tongue of Ra. Antebu [is] the guide of the two lands. Geb is established [through] his rudders. The power that opens the Disk. The prince of red beings, I am brought as the one who was shipwrecked; may he grant that my khu, my brother, may come to me, and that [I] may depart to the place that you know."

"Tell me my name," says the Wood where I would anchor; "Lord of the two lands that dwell in the Sanctuary," that is your name.

"Tell me my name," says the Rudder; "Leg of Hapi," that is your name.

"Tell me my name," says the Rope; "Hair with which Anpu (Anubis) finishes the work of my embalming," that is your name.

"Tell us our name," say the Rowing Supports; "Pillars of the Underworld," that is your name.

"Tell me my name," says the Fortress; "Akar," that is your name.

"Tell me my name," says the Mast; "The one who brings back the great lady after she is gone", that is your name.

"Tell me my name," says the Lower Deck; "Pattern of Ap-uat," that is your name.

"Tell me my name," says the Upper Deck; "Throat of Mestha," that is your name.

"Tell me my name," says the Canvas; "Nut," that is your name.

"Tell us our name," say the Pieces of Leather; "You that are made of the leather of the Bull Mnevis, which was burned by Suti," that is your name.

"Tell us our name," say the Oars; "Fingers of Horus, the firstborn," that is your name.

"Tell me my name," says Matchabet; "The hand of Isis, which wipes the blood from the Eye of Horus," that is your name.

"Tell us our names," say the Planks that are in its hull; "Imsety, Hapi, Duamutef, Qebehsenuef, Haqau (i.e., the one who takes captive), Thet-em-aua (i.e., the one who seizes by violence, Maa-an-tef (i.e., the one who sees what the father brings), and Ari-nef-t-chesef (that is, the one who made himself)," these are your names.

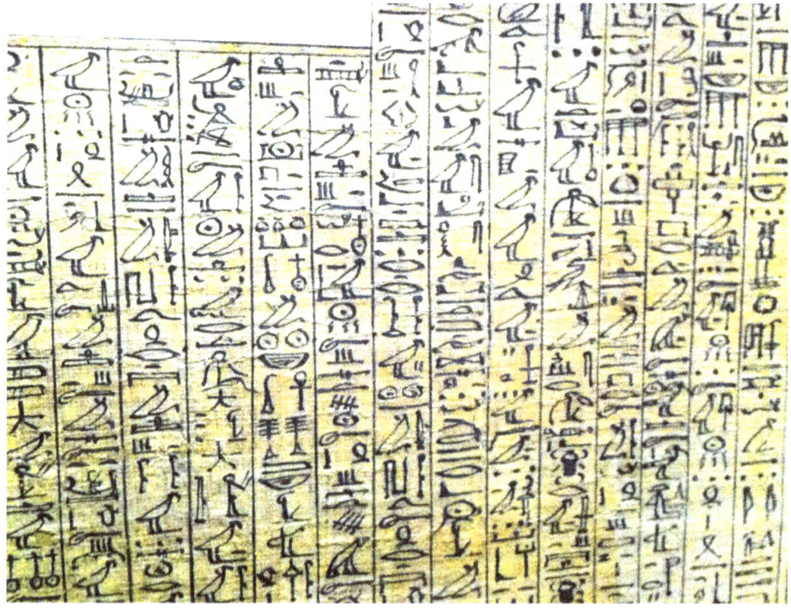

Detail of a funerary book.

"Tell us our name," say the Arches; "The one that is in front of your name," that is your name.

"Tell me my name," says the Hull; "Mert," that is your name.

"Tell me my name," says the Rudder; "Aqa," (i.e., true) that is your name, oh, you who shine from the water, hidden ray, that is your name.

"Tell me my name," says the Keel; "Thigh (or Leg) of Isis, which Ra cut with the knife to bring blood to the boat Sektet," that is your name.

"Tell me my name," says the Sailor; "Traveler," that is your name.

"Tell me my name," says the Wind by which you are carried; "The North Wind that comes from Tem to the nostrils of Khenti-Amenti," that is your name.

"Tell me my name," says the River, "if you want to travel over me;" "The one who can be seen," that is your name.

"Tell us our name," say the Shores; "Destroyer of the god Au-a (that is, the one of the illusory hands) in the house of water," that is your name.

"Tell me my name," says the Floor, "if you want to walk on me;" "The Nose of the sky that proceeds from the god Utu, who dwells in Sekhet-Aaru, and who comes out of it with rejoicing," that is your name.

THEN THESE WORDS WILL BE RECITED BEFORE THEM:

"Hail you, oh, divine beings with splendid kas, oh, divine lords of things, who exist and who live forever, and [whose] double period of an unlimited number of years is eternity, I made a way until you, grant me food and sepulchral food for my mouth, [and grant that] I may speak with it, and that the goddess Isis [may give me] bread and cakes in the presence of the great god. I know the great god before whose nostrils you place tchefau food, and his name is Thekem; both when he makes his way from the eastern horizon of the sky and when he travels to the western horizon of the sky, let his journey be my journey, and his coming forth, my coming forth. May I not be destroyed in the chamber of Mesqet, and may demons not dominate my limbs. I have my cakes in the city of Pe, and I have my beer in the city of Tepu, and may the offerings [given to you] be given to me today. May my offerings be wheat and barley; may my offerings be ointment and linen clothes; may my offerings be for life, strength and health: may my offerings appear by day in any form I please to appear in Sekhet-Aaru".

IF THIS CHAPTER IS KNOWN [BY THE DECEASED] IT WILL COME FORTH TO SEKHET-AARRU, AND BREAD, WINE, AND CAKES WILL BE GIVEN TO IT ON THE ALTAR OF THE GREAT GOD, AND FIELDS AND A PROPERTY [SOWN] WITH WHEAT AND BARLEY, WHICH THE FOLLOWERS OF HORUS WILL HARVEST FOR IT. AND IT WILL EAT OF THIS WHEAT AND BARLEY, AND ITS LIMBS WILL BE NOURISHED WITH THAT, AND ITS BODY WILL BE LIKE THE BODIES OF THE GODS, AND IT WILL COME FORTH TO SEKHET-AARU IN ANY FORM IT WANTS, AND IT WILL APPEAR THEREBY REGULARLY AND CONTINUOUSLY.

Of Entering the Boat of Ra

[From the Papyrus of Nu (British Museum Nu 10477, sheets 27 and 28)].

THE BOOK OF MAKING THE KHU PERFECT AND MAKING IT GO TO THE BOAT OF RA ALONG WITH THOSE WHO ARE IN ITS ACCOMPANIMENT (?). The superintendent of the palace, the chancellor-in-chief, Nu, triumphant, said:

"I brought the divine Bennu to the east, and Osiris to the city of Tattu. I opened the treasure houses of the god Hapi, cleaned the roads of the (solar) Disk, and dragged the god Sekeri on his sled. The powerful and divine Lady strengthened me in her hour. I praised and glorified the Disk, and I joined the divine monkeys who sing at dawn, and I am a divine Being among them. I made myself a counterpart of the goddess Isis, and her power (khu) made me strong. I tied the rope, made Apep retreat, made him walk backwards. Ra reached out both hands to me, and his sailors did not repel me; my strength is the strength of Utchat, and the strength of Utchat is my strength. If the superintendent of the house, the chancellor-in-chief, Nu, triumphant, is separated [from the boat of Ra], then he (i.e., Ra) will be separated from the Egg and the fish Abtu."

THIS CHAPTER WILL BE RECITED OVER THE DRAWING ABOVE AND WRITTEN ON VIRGIN PAPYRUS, WITH [INK MADE OF] GREEN GRAINS MIXED WITH WATER, AND THE PAPYRUS WILL BE PLACED ON THE CHEST OF THE DECEASED; IT MUST NOT ENTER TO (I.E., TOUCH) ITS LIMBS. IF THIS IS DONE FOR ANY DECEASED, IT WILL GO FORTH IN THE BOAT OF RA IN THE COURSE OF THE DAY EVERY DAY, AND THE GOD THOTH WILL TAKE ACCOUNT OF IT AS IT COMES FORTH AND GOES IN THE COURSE OF THE DAY EVERY DAY, REGULARLY AND CONTINUOUS-LY, [IN THE BOAT OF RA] AS A PERFECT KHU. And it will put on the TET and sail with RA anywhere it wants.

Of Protecting the Boat of Ra

[From the Papyrus of Nu (British Museum N 10477, sheet 27)].
[THE CHAPTER OF PROTECTING THE BOAT OF RA].

"Oh, you, who cut the water when you come out of the stream and sit in your place in your boat, sit in your place in your boat when you go out to your station of yesterday, and join Osiris and the superinten-dent of the palace, the chancellor-in-chief, Nu, triumphant, the perfect khu, to your sailors, and may their strength be your strength. Hail, Ra, in your name of Ra, if you pass through the eye of seven cubits, which

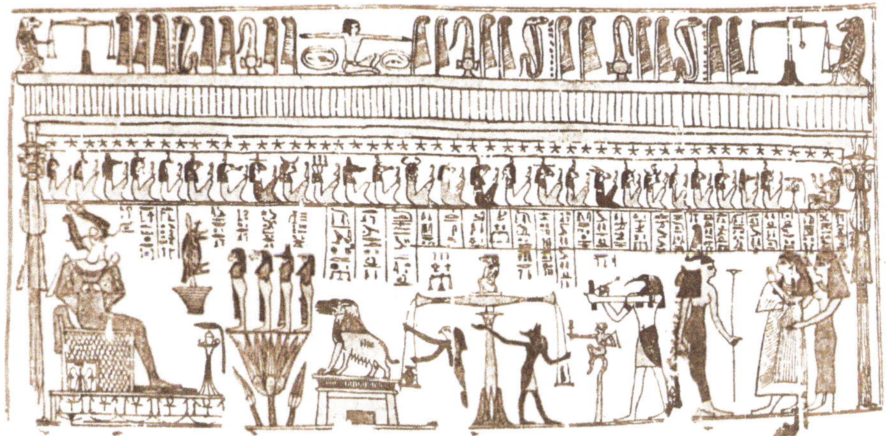

Page of a *Book of the Dead* showing the judgment of souls by Osiris.

Detail of a funerary book.

has a pupil of three cubits, then you truly strengthen Osiris, Nu, triumphant, the perfect khu, [and may he be among] your sailors, and may your strength be their strength. Hail, Ra, in your name of Ra, if you pass by those who are overthrown in death, then you truly cause Osiris, Nu, triumphant, the perfect soul, to stand, and may your strength be their strength. Hail, Ra, in your name of Ra, if the hidden things of the underworld are opened to you, and you gratify the heart of the cycle of your gods, then you truly grant joy of heart to the chancellor-in-chief, Nu, triumphant, and let your strength be his strength. Your limbs, oh, Ra, are established by (this) Chapter."

[THIS CHAPTER] MUST BE RECITED OVER A FINE LINEN STRIP, WHICH WILL BE PLACED ON THE NECK OF THE DECEASED FOR THE PERFECT KHU ON THE DAY OF BURIAL. IF THIS AMULET IS PUT ON ITS NECK, IT WILL DO EVERYTHING IT WANTS TO DO LIKE THE GODS; AND IT WILL JOIN THE FOLLOWERS OF HORUS; AND IT WILL BE ESTABLISHED AS A STAR, FACE TO FACE WITH SOPDET (SOTIS); AND ITS CORRUPTIBLE BODY WILL BE FOREVER LIKE A GOD ALONG WITH ITS PARTNERS; AND THE GODDESS MESKHENET WILL MAKE PLANTS TO GERMINATE IN ITS BODY; AND THE MAJESTY OF THE GOD THOTH, WITH LOVE, MAKES THE LIGHT TO REST AT THE WILL OF ITS CORRUPTIBLE BODY, AS HE DID FOR THE MAJESTY OF THE KING OF THE NORTH AND SOUTH, THE GOD OSIRIS, TRIUMPHANT.

Of Going into the Boat of Ra

[From the Papyrus of Nu (British Museum N 10477, sheet 28)].

THE CHAPTER OF GOING INTO THE BOAT OF RA. The chancellor-in-chief, Nu, triumphant, said:

"Hail, great God who is in your boat, bring me to your boat. [I approached your steps], let me be the director of your journeys, and let me be among those who belong to you and who are among the stars that never rest. What is an abomination to you and what is an abomination to me, I will not eat; what is an abomination to me, what is an abomination to me is filth, and I will not eat it; but sepulchral offerings and sacred foods [I will eat], and I will not be overthrown for it. I will not approach filth with my hands, I will not walk on it with my sandals, because my bread [is made] of white barley, and my beer [is made] of red barley; and behold, the boat Sektet and the boat Matet brought these things, and laid the gifts of the lands on the altar of the Souls of Anu. Hymns of praise be to you, oh, Ur-arit-s, as you travel through the sky! May there be food [for you], oh, dweller of the city of Teni, and when the dogs gather together, do not let me suffer harm. I myself came and freed the god from the things that were inflicted on him, and from the serious illness of the body, of his arm and leg. I came and spat on the body, tied the arm and made the leg walk. [I] entered [the boat] and sail ed by the command of Ra."

Of Knowing the Souls of the East

[From the Papyrus of Nu (British Museum N 10477, sheet 12)].

THE CHAPTER OF KNOWING THE SOULS OF THE EAST. The chancellor-in-chief, Nu, triumphant, said:

"I, myself, know the eastern gate of heaven. I know that its southern part is in the lake of Kharu and its northern part is in the Canal of Geese, from where Ra comes with winds that make him advance. I am the one who cares about the equipment [that is] on the divine boat, I am the sailor who does not stop in the boat of Ra.

I, myself, I know the two turquoise sycamores between which Ra shows himself when he advances over the supports of Shu towards the gate of the Lord of the East through which Ra comes forth. I, myself, I know the Sektet-Aaru of Ra, whose walls are made of iron. The height of the wheat in it is five cubits, of its ears two cubits, and of its stems three cubits. The barley in it is seven cubits high, its ears are three cubits, and its stems are four cubits. And behold, the khus, each of which is nine cubits high, are gathered near the divine Souls of the East. I, myself, know the divine Souls of the East, that is, Herukhuti (Harmachis), and the Calf of the goddess Khera, and the Morning Star [daily. A divine city was built for me, I know it and I know its name: 'Sekhet-Aaru' is its name]."

Of Sekhet-Hetepet

[From the Papyrus of Nebseni (British Museum N 9900, sheet 17)].

HERE BEGIN THE CHAPTERS OF SEKHET-HETEPET, AND THE CHAPTERS OF COMING FORTH BY DAY; OF ENTERING AND LEAVING THE UNDERWORLD; OF COMING TO SEKHET-AARU; OF BEING IN SEKHET-HETEPET, THE MIGHTY LAND, THE LADY OF THE WINDS; OF HAVING POWER THERE; OF BECOMING A KHU THERE; OF PLOWING THERE; OF HARVESTING THERE; OF EATING THERE; OF DRINKING THERE; OF MAKING LOVE THERE; AND OF DOING EVERYTHING AS A MAN DOES ON EARTH. Here is the scribe and artist of the Temple of Ptah, Nebseni, who says:

"Set took possession of Horus, who looked with both eyes at the building around Sekhet-Hetepet, but I freed Horus [and took him

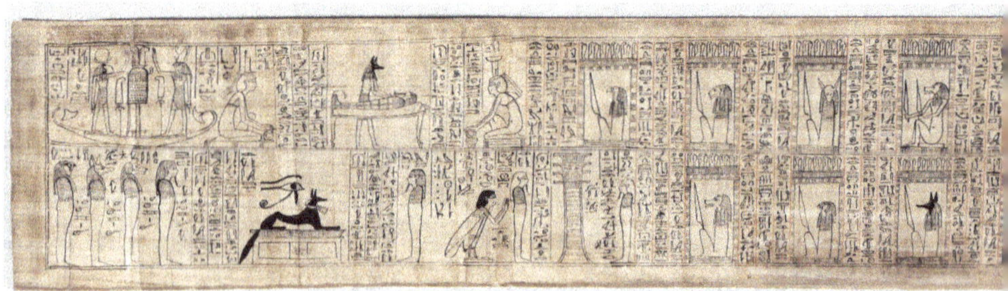

from] Set, and Set opened the paths of both eyes [which are] in heaven. Set cast his moisture to the winds over the soul [that has] his day (or his eye) and that dwells in the city of Mert, and he freed the inside of the body of Horus from the gods of Akert. See me now, for I made this mighty boat to travel upon the Lake of Hetepet, and I brought it in strength from the palace of Shu; the mastery of his stars rejuvenates and renews his former strength. I brought the boat to his lakes so that I could go out to his cities, and I sailed to his divine city, Hetepet. And behold, it is because I, myself, am at peace with his seasons, and with his guidance, and with his territory, and with the company of the gods who are his firstborn. He causes the two divine fighters (that is, Horus and Set) to be in peace with those who watch over the living that he created in a fair way, and he brings peace [with him]; he causes the two divine fighters to be in peace with those who watch over them. He cuts the hair of divine warriors, he drives away the storm from the defenseless, and he keeps evil away from the khus. Let me gain the mastery within this field, for I know it, and I sailed among his lakes to enter his cities. My mouth is strong; and I am equipped [with weapons to use] against the khus; let them not have mastery over me. Let me be rewarded with your fields, oh, you, god of Hetepet; what is your wish, you will do, oh, lord of the winds. May I become a khu therein, may I eat therein, may I drink therein, may I plow therein, may I harvest therein, may I fight therein, may I make love therein, may my words be powerful therein, may I never be in a state of servitude in it, but that I may be in authority in it. You made strong the mouth and throat of the god of Hetepet; Qetetbu is his name. He is established over the watery supports of the god Shu, and is connected with the pleasant things of Ra. He is the divider of years, he is hidden from the mouth, his mouth is

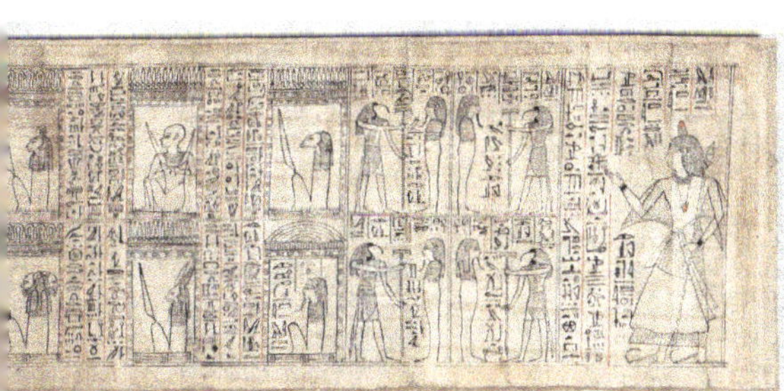

The *Book of the Dead* of the priest Hori, excerpt from the *Book of Gates*. There are sixteen gates that Hori must pass through, each guarded by a fierce monster, with an animal head and wielding a dagger.

silent; what he utters is secret, he fulfills eternity and takes possession of the eternity of existence as lord of Hetepet. The god Horus becomes strong like the falcon that is a thousand cubits long and two thousand [cubits wide] in life; he has equipment with him, and he travels back and forth wherever his heart wants in his lakes and in his cities. He was begotten in the birth chamber of the city god, he has offerings [made to him] of the food of the city god, he performs what is proper to do there, and the union of this, in the matter of all the birth chambers of the divine city. When [he] establishes life as a crystal, he performs everything in it, and these things are similar to the things that are done in the Lake of Double Fire, where there is no one who rejoices and where there are all kinds of evil things. The god of Hetepet enters and leaves, and retreats [in] the Field that gathers all kinds of things to the birth chamber of the city god. When he establishes life as a crystal, he performs all kinds of things in it that are similar to the things that are done in the Lake of Double Fire, where there is no one who rejoices, and where there are evil things. [Let me] live with the god of Hetepet, clothed and not despoiled by the lords of the north, and may the lords of divine things bring me food; may he bring me forward and may I go forth, and may he bring my power to me there, and may I receive it, and may my equipment be of the god of Hetepet. May I gain mastery over the great and powerful word that is in my body in this place of mine, and by doing so, I will remember and forget. Let me go forward on my journey, and let me plow. I am in peace in the divine city, and I know the waters, cities, nomes and lakes that are in Sekhet-Hetepet. I

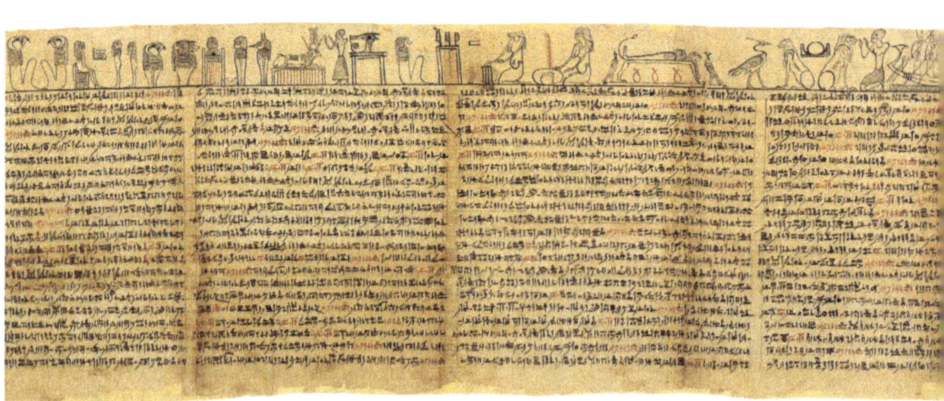

exist therein, I am strong therein, I become a khu therein, I eat therein, I sow therein, I plow therein, I harvest therein, I make love therein, I am in peace with the god of Hetepet. Behold, there I scatter the seed, I sail between your lakes and advance to your cities, oh, divine Hetepet. Behold, my mouth is equipped with my horns [for teeth]. Grant me an overflowing supply of food over which the kas and khus [live]. I made the judgment of Shu on the one who knows him, so that I may go to his cities, and may sail among his lakes, and walk in Sekhet-Hetepet; and behold, Ra is in the sky, and behold, the god of Hetepet is his double offering. I came to his land, I put on my belt, I came so that the gifts that were about to be given to me might be given, I rejoiced for my-self. I clung to my strength, which the god of Hetepet greatly increased for me. Oh, Unen-em-hetepet, I entered you and my soul follows me, and my divine food is in my two hands, oh, Lady of the two lands, who establishes my word by which I remember and forget; I would live without injury, without any injury [being done] to me, oh, grant me, oh, grant me joy of heart. Make me be at peace, tie my tendons and muscles, and make me receive air. Oh, Un[en]-em-hetepet, Lady of the winds, I entered you and opened (that is, showed) my head. Ra falls asleep, but I am awake, and there is the goddess Hast at the gate of the sky at night. Obstacles were placed before me, but I gathered what he issued. I am in my city. Oh, Nut-urt, I entered you and counted my harvest, and I go forward to Uakh. I am the Bull wrapped in turquoise, the lord of the Bull Field, the lord of the divine speech of the goddess Sopdet (Sotis) in her hours. Oh, Uakh, I entered you, I ate my bread, I

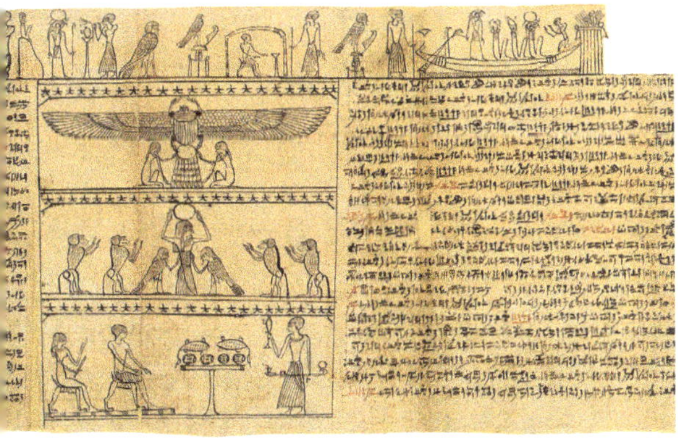

The *Book of the Dead* of Imhotep, priest of Horus.

acquired the mastery over choice pieces of meat from oxen and feathered birds, and the birds of Shu were given to me; I follow the gods and [I follow] the divine kas. Oh, Tchefet, I entered you. I dress myself in clothes, and I dress myself with the garment of Ra; now see, [he is] in the sky, and those who dwell in it follow Ra, and [I] follow Ra in the sky. Oh, Unen-em-hetepet, lord of the two lands, I entered you and dove into the lakes of Tchesert; here I am, for all filth was moved away from me. The Great God grows in it, and behold, I found [food in it]; I trapped the feathered birds and fed on the best [of them]. Oh, Qenqentet, I entered you, and I saw Osiris [my father], and I beheld my mother, and I made love. I caught the worms and the serpents, and I am free. And I know the name of the god who is opposite to the goddess of Tchesert, and who has straight hair and is equipped with two horns; he reaps, and I wash and reap. Oh, Hast, I entered you, drove away those who wanted to come to the turquoise sky, and followed the winds of the company of the gods. The Great God gave my head to me, and the one who tied my head to me is the Mighty One who has turquoise eyes. Oh, Usert, I entered you in the head of the house, where divine food is brought to me. Oh, Smam, I entered you. My heart watches, my head is equipped with the white crown, I am carried to the heavenly regions, and I cause earthly objects to flourish, and there is joy of heart for the Bull, for the heavenly beings, and for the company of the gods. I am the god who is the Bull, the lord of the gods, as he comes out of the turquoise [sky]. Oh, divine nome of wheat and barley, I came to you, I approached you and accepted what follows me, that is, the best of libations from the company of the gods. I tied my boat in the heavenly lakes, raised the pole to anchor, recited the prescribed words with my voice, and assigned praises to the gods who dwell in Sekhet-Hetepet."

Of Knowing the Souls of Pe

[From the Papyrus of Nu (British Museum N 10477, sheet 18)].

ANOTHER CHAPTER OF KNOWING THE SOULS OF PE. The superintendent of the palace, the chancellor-in-chief, Nu, triumphant, says: "[Hail,] Khat, who dwells in Khat, in Anpet, and in the nome of Khat! [Hail,] you goddesses of the hunt who dwell in the city

The *Book of the Dead* of Imhotep, priest of Horus; detail of Apep,
here as a crocodile, being harpooned.

of Pe, you heavenly lands, you stars, and you divine beings, who give cakes and beer; do you know why the city of Pe was given to Horus? I, myself, know, although you do not know. Behold, Ra gave him the city in exchange for the wound in his eye, which is why Ra said to Horus: 'Let me see what is happening in your eye,' and immediately he looked at it. Then Ra said to Horus: 'Look at that black pig,' and he looked, and immediately a wound was made in its eye, [that is] a strong storm [took place]. Then Horus said to Ra: 'Truly, my eye seems as if it was an eye on which Suti inflicted a blow;' [and thus saying] he ate its heart. Then Ra said to those gods: 'Put him in his room, and he will do well.' Now the black pig was Suti who turned into a black pig, and it was he who aimed the blow of fire that was in the eye of Horus. Then Ra said to those gods: 'The pig is an abominable thing to Horus; oh, but he will do well, although the pig is an abomination to him.' Then the company of the gods, who were among the divine followers of Horus when he existed in the form of his own son, said: 'Let sacrifices be made [to the gods] of his bulls, and of his goats, and of and of his pigs'. Now the father of Imsety, Hapi, Duamutef, and Qebehsenuef is Horus, and their mother is Isis. Then Horus said to Ra: 'Give

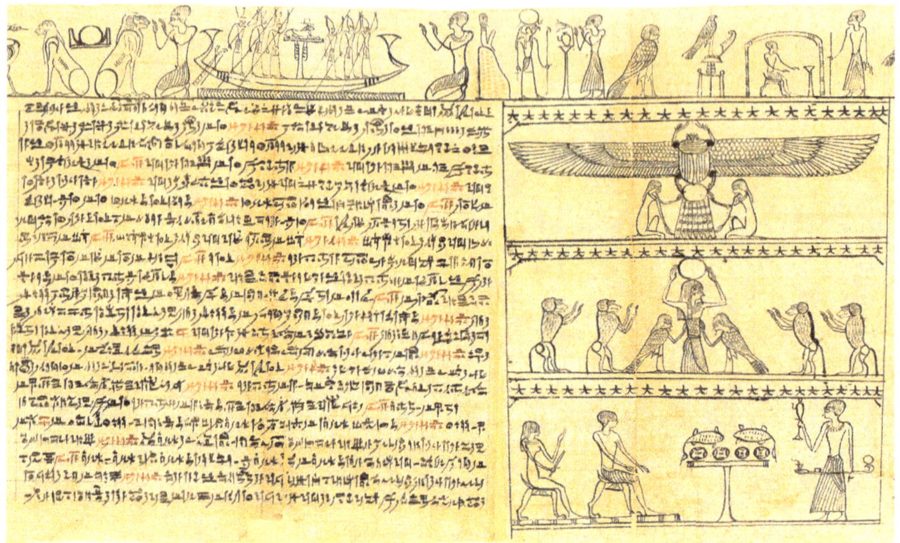

Detail of the funerary book of Imhotep.

me two divine brothers in the city of Pe and two divine brothers in the city of Nekhen, who [arose] from my body and who will be with me in the form of eternal judges, then the earth will flourish and the clouds of thunder and the rain will be blotted out'. And the name of Horus became 'Her-uatch-f' (that is, Prince of His Emerald Stone). I, myself, know the Souls of Pe, that is, Horus, Imsety and Hapi."

Of Knowing the Souls of Nekhen

[From the Papyrus of Nu (British Museum N 10477, sheet 18)].

THE CHAPTER OF KNOWING THE SOULS OF NEKHEN. The superintendent of the palace, the chancellor-in-chief, Nu, triumphant, says:

"I know the hidden things of the city of Nekhen, that is, the things that the mother of Horus did for him, and how she [made her voice come out] over the waters, saying: 'Tell me about the judgment that is upon me, [and show me] the way behind you, and let me discover it'; and as Ra said: 'This son of Isis perished'; and what the mother of Horus did for him [when] she cried out, saying: 'Sobek, the lord of the papyrus swamp, will be brought to us.' [And Sobek] fished for them and found them, and the mother of Horus made them grow up in the places where they belonged. Then Sobek, the lord of his papyrus swamp, said: 'I went and found the place where they had passed with my fingers at the edge of the waters, and I wrapped them in [my] net: and strong was that net.' And Ra said: 'Then there are fish with the god Sobek, and [he] found the hands and arms of Horus for him in the land of fish;' and [that] land became the land of the city of Remu (that is, Fish). And Ra said: 'A land of the Lake, a land of the Lake for this net.' Then the hands of Horus were brought to him by uncovering his face in the festivals of the month and half month in the Land of Remu. And Ra said: 'I give the city of Nekhen to Horus for the dwelling of his two arms and hands, and his face will be uncovered before his two hands and arms in the city of Nekhen; and I deliver in his power the slaughtered beings that are therein in the festivals of the month and half month.' Then Horus said: 'Let me take Duamutef

Detail of the funerary book of Kenna.

and Qebehsenuef, and let them watch over my body; and if they can be there, then they will be subservient to the god of the city of Nekhen.' And Ra said: 'It will be granted to you there and in the city of Sekhet, and it will be done for them as was done for those who dwell in the city of Nekhen, and verily they will be with you.' And Horus said: 'They were with you, and [now] they will be with me, and will hear the god Suti when he invokes the Souls of Nekhen.' Grant me [that I, myself, I may pass to the Souls of Nekhen, and that I may lose the bonds of Horus]. I, myself, I know the Souls of Nekhen, that is, Horus, Duamutef and Qebehsenuef."

Of Knowing the Souls of Khmunu

[From the Papyrus of Nebseni (British Museum N 9900, sheet 7)].

THE CHAPTER OF KNOWING THE SOULS OF KHMUNU (Hermopolis).

"The goddess Maat is carried by the arm in the brightness of the goddess Neith in the city of Mentchat, and in the brightness of the Eye when it is weighed. I am carried away by it and I know what it brings from the city of Kesi, and I will not declare it to men nor tell it to the gods. I came, being the envoy of Ra, to establish Maat over the arm of the radiance of Neith in the city of Mentchat and to grant the eye to the one who should examine it. I came as a power through the knowledge of the Souls of Khmunu (Hermopolis) who love to know what you love. I know Maat, who germinated and became

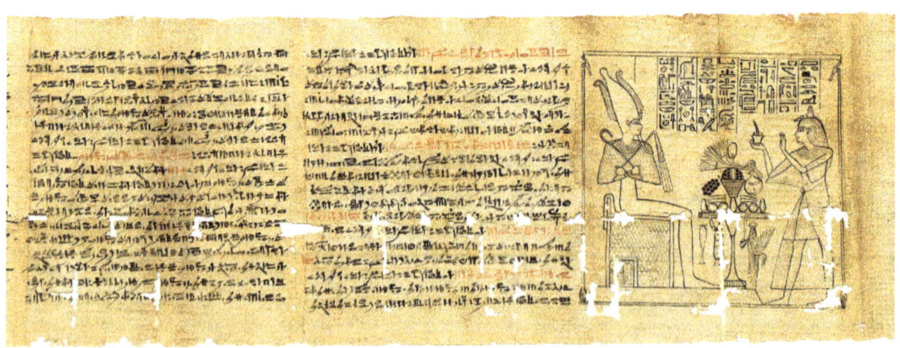

Funerary papyrus of Nesiamun.

strong and was judged, and I have joy in judging the things that are to be judged. Homage to you, oh, Souls of Khmunu, I, myself, know the things that are unknown in the festivals of the month and half month. Ra knows the hidden things of the night, and knows that it was Thoth who made me have knowledge. Homage to you, oh, Souls of Khmunu, as I know you every day."

Of Coming Forth from Heaven

[From the Papyrus of Nu (British Museum N 10477, sheet 18)].

THE CHAPTER OF COMING FORTH FROM HEAVEN, AND OF MAKING A WAY THROUGH AMENTET, AND OF KNOWING THE SOULS OF ANU (HELIOPOLIS). The chancellor-in-chief, Nu, triumphant, said:

"I spent the day since yesterday among the great divine beings, and I came into existence together with the god Khepri. [My] face is uncovered before the Eye, the Only One, and the orbit of the night is opened. I am a divine being among you. I know the Souls of Anu. Will not the god Ur-ma pass by it as [he] travels forward with vigor? Did I not win, and did I not speak to the gods? See, the one who is the heir of Anu was destroyed. I, myself, know for what reason the lock of hair of the Man was made. Ra spoke to the god Ami-haf, and a wound was made in his mouth, that is, he was wounded [in that] mouth. And Ra spoke to the god Ami-haf, saying: 'Oh, heir of men, receive [your] harpoon;' and the house of the harpoon arose. Behold, oh, god Ami-haf, two divine brothers arose, [that is], Senti-Ra arose and Setem-ansi-f arose. And his hand did not stop, and he made his form into that of a woman with a lock of hair which became the divine lock in Anu, and which became strong and powerful in this temple; and it became the strong one of Anu, and it became the heir of the heir of Ur-maat-f (that is, the mighty one of the two eyes), and it became before him the god Urma of Anu. I know the Souls of Anu, that is, Ra, Shu and Tefnut."

Of Knowing the Souls of Khmunu

[From the Papyrus of Nu (British Museum N 10477, sheet 18)].

ANOTHER CHAPTER OF KNOWING THE SOULS OF KHMUNU (HERMOPOLIS). The chancellor-in-chief, Nu, triumphant, said:

"The goddess Neith shines in Matchat, and the goddess Maat is carried by the arm of the one who eats the Eye, and who is her divine judge, and the priest Sem carries me over him. I will not declare it to men or to gods; I will not declare it to men and I will not tell it to the gods. I entered as an ignorant man and saw hidden things. Homage to you, oh, gods who dwell in Khmunu, you know me as I know the goddess Neith, and [you give] to the Eye the growth that endures. There is joy [for me] in the judgment of the things that are to be judged. I, myself, know the Souls of Anu; they are great in the festival of the month and they are small in the festival of the half month. They are Thoth, the Hidden One, and Sa, and Tem."

IF THIS CHAPTER IS KNOWN [BY THE DECEASED], THE OFFAL WILL BE AN ABOMINATION TO THEM, AND THEY WILL NOT DRINK FILTHY WATER.

The weighing of the heart, in the *Book of the Dead* of Kenna.

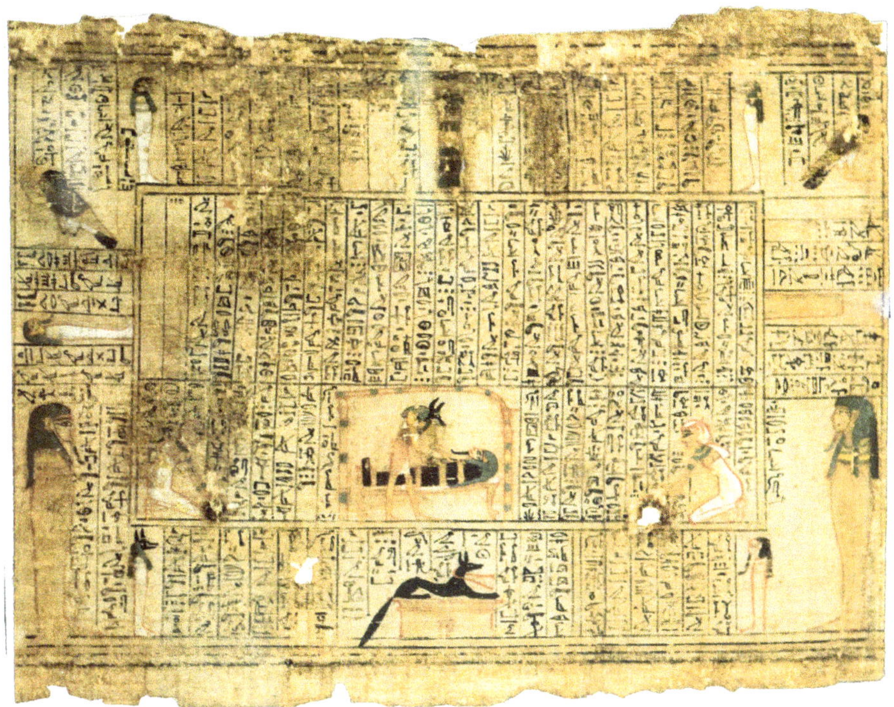

Detail of the funerary book of Kenna.

Of Receiving Paths

[From the Papyrus of Nu (British Museum N 10477, sheet 9)].

THE CHAPTER OF RECEIVING PATHS [WHERE TO WALK] IN RE-STAU. The chancellor-in-chief, Nu, triumphant, said:

"The paths that are above me [lead] to Re-stau. I am the one who is girded with his belt and who comes out of the [goddess of] the Uraeus crown. I came and established things in Abtu (Abydos), and opened paths in Re-stau. The god Osiris eased my pain. I am the one who makes the waters come into existence, and who establishes his throne [here], and who makes his path through the burial valley and through the Great Lake. I made my path, and indeed I am [Osiris]."

"[Osiris was victorious over his enemies, and Osiris Nebqet is victorious over his enemies. He became one of you [oh, gods], his protector is the Lord of eternity, he walks as you walk, he stands as you stand, he sits as you sit, and he speaks as you speak in the presence of the Great God, the Lord of Amentet]."

Detail of the funerary book of Kenna, with Ammit, the devourer of souls.

Of Coming Forth from Re-Stau I

[From the Papyrus of Nu (British Museum N 10477, sheet 9)].

THE CHAPTER OF COMING FORTH FROM RE-STAU. The chancellor-in-chief, Nu, triumphant, said:

"I was born in Re-stau, and splendor was given to me by those who dwell in their spiritual bodies (sahu) in the dwelling where libations are made to Osiris. The divine ministers who are in Re-stau must receive [me] when Osiris is led to the double burial region of Osiris; oh, let me be a divine being to whom they will lead to the double burial region of Osiris."

Of Coming Forth from Re-Stau II

[From the Papyrus of Nu (British Museum N 10477, sheet 9)].

THE CHAPTER OF COMING FORTH FROM RE-STAU. The chancellor-in-chief, Nu, triumphant, said:

"I am the Great Name that makes your light. I came to you, oh, Osiris, and I offer praise to you. [I am] pure from the issues that are taken away from you. Your name is made in Re-stau, and your power is in Abtu (Abydos). You are raised up, then, oh, Osiris, and you traverse the sky with Ra, and you look upon the generations of men, oh, you, The One who circles, you, Ra. Behold, in truth, I said to you, oh, Osiris: 'I am the spiritual body of the God,' and I say: 'May it come to pass that I shall never be repelled before you, oh, Osiris.'"

The following is the chapter in a more complete form:

THE CHAPTER OF KNOWING THE NAME OF OSIRIS AND OF GOING IN AND COMING FORTH FROM RE-STAU [IN ALL THE FORMS IN WHICH HE WANTS TO COME FORTH]. The scribe Mes-em-neter, triumphant, says:

"I am the Great Name that makes your light. I came to you, oh, Osiris, and I offer praise to you. I am pure from the issues that are taken away from you. [Your] name was made in Re-stau when it fell therein. Homage to you, oh, Osiris, in your strength and in your power, you obtained the mastery in Re-stau. You are raised up, oh, Osiris, in your strength and in your power, you are raised up, oh, Osiris, and your power is in Re-stau, and your power is in Abtu (Abydos). You go round through the sky, and you sail before Ra, and you look at the generations of men, oh, you, a Being who circles, you, Ra. Behold, in truth, I said to you, oh, Osiris: 'I am the spiritual body of the God,' and I say: 'May it come to pass that I shall never be repelled before you, oh, Osiris.'"

Walking in the Underworld

[From the Papyrus of Nu (British Museum N 10477, sheet 9)].

THE CHAPTER OF GOING IN AFTER COMING FORTH [THE UNDERWORLD]. The superintendent of the palace, the chancellor-in-chief, Nu, triumphant, said:

"Open for me? Who, then, are you? Where are you going? What is your name? I am one of you, 'The One Who Gathers Souls' is the name of my boat; 'Making the hair stand on end' is the name of the

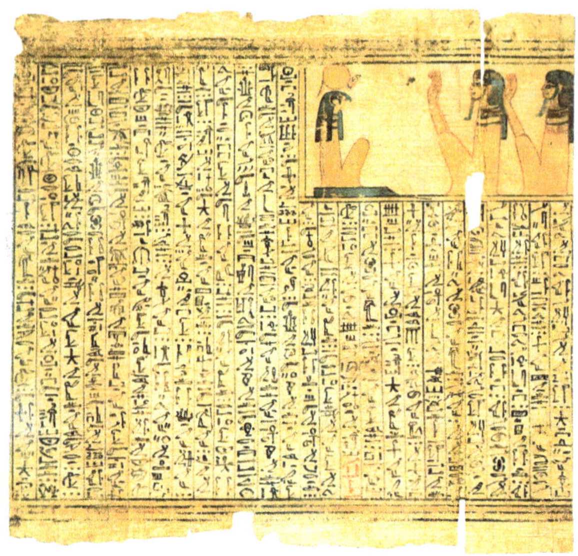

The *Book of the Dead* of Kenna, the only one to include a passage describing the activity of a soul in an afterlife location, the House of Hearts.

oars; 'Watchful One' is the name of its arches; 'Evil is it' is the name of the rudder; 'Steering straight to the middle' is the name of Match-abet; in the same way [the boat] is a type of my sailing to the Lake. May vessels of milk be given to me, together with cakes and bread, and glasses of drink and pieces of meat in the Temple of Anpu," or (as others say): "Grant me [these things] in full. Let it be done for me that I may go in like a falcon, and that I may come forth like the bird Bennu, [and like] the Morning Star. Let me make [my] path so that [I] may go in peace to beautiful Amentet, and let the Lake of Osiris be mine. Let me make my path, and let me go in, and let me worship Osiris, the Lord of life."

Entering the Great House

From the Papyrus of Nu (British Museum N 10477, sheet 10)].

THE CHAPTER OF ENTERING THE GREAT HOUSE. The superintendent of the palace, the chancellor-in-chief, Nu, triumphant, said:

"Homage to you, oh, Thoth. I am Thoth, who weighed the two divine fighters (that is, Horus and Set). I destroyed their war and lessened their lamentations. I freed the fish Atu in its return, and I fulfilled what you commanded concerning it, and then I lay down within my eye. [I am the one who was without opposition. I came; look at me in the Temple of Nem-hra (or Uhem-hra)]. I give orders in the words of the divine elders, and, furthermore, I guide the lesser deities for you."

Entering the Presence

[From the Papyrus of Nu (British Museum N 10477, sheet 10)].

THE CHAPTER OF ENTERING THE PRESENCE OF THE DIVINE SOVEREIGN PRINCES OF OSIRIS. The superintendent of the palace, the chancellor-in-chief, Nu, triumphant, said:

"My soul built for me a dwelling in the city of Tattu; I sow in the city of Pe, and I plow my field with my workers, and therefore my palm tree is like Amsu. What is an abomination to me, what is an abomination to me, I will not eat. What is an abomination to me, what is an abomination to me is filth. I will not eat of it; by sepulchral meals and food I will not be destroyed. [The abominable thing] I will not take in my hands, I will not walk on it with my sandals, because my breads are [made] of white

Detail of the Book of the Dead of Kenna.

grain, and my beer is [made] of red grain; and behold, the boat Sektet and the boat Matet bring them to me, and I eat [of them] under the branches of [trees], the beautiful arms [of which] I know. Oh, may splendor be prepared for me with the white crown that is raised upon me by the uræi goddesses. Hail, guardian of the divine doors of the god Sehetep-taui (that is, 'the one who makes the world to be in peace'), may [you] bring to me that of which they make sepulchral meals; grant me that I may lift the branches. May the god of light open his arms to me, and may the company of the gods be silent while the inhabitants of heaven talk to the chancellor-in-chief, Nu, triumphant. I am the leader of the hearts of the gods that strengthen me, and I am a mighty one among divine beings. If any god or goddess comes against me, they will be judged by the ancestors of the year who live on hearts and who make cakes for me, and Osiris must devour them coming forth from Abtu (Abydos). They will be judged by the ancestors of Ra and will be judged by the God of Light who dresses the sky among the divine princes. I will have bread in my mouth at certain seasons, and I will enter before the gods, Ahiu. He will talk to me and I will talk to the followers of the gods. I will talk to the Disk, and I will talk to the

Detail of the Book of the Dead of Kenna

The Book of the Dead of Kenna, from the collection of the Rijksmuseum, Netherlands.

inhabitants of heaven. I will place the terror of myself in the darkness of the night that is in the goddess Meh-urt, [who is near] of the one who dwells in power. And behold, I will be there with Osiris. My condition of completeness will be his condition of completeness among the divine princes. I will talk to him [with] the words of men, and he will repeat to me the words of the gods. A khu equipped [with power] will come. I am a khu equipped [with power]; I am equipped [with the power] of all khus, [being the form of the Sahu (that is, spiritual bodies) of Anu, Tattu, Suten-henen, Abtu, Apu and Sennu. The Osiris Auf-ankh is victorious over every god and goddess who are hidden in Neter-khertet]."

The Introduction to Maat I
[From the Papyrus of Ani (British Museum N 10470, sheet 30)].

THE CHAPTER OF ENTERING THE HALL OF MAAT; A HYMN OF PRAISE TO OSIRIS, THE GOVERNOR OF AMENTET. Osiris, the scribe Ani, triumphant, says:

"I came and [approached] to see your beauties; my hands [are raised] in worship of your name, 'Righteousness and Truth.' Neither herb nor grass. Then I entered the hidden place, and spoke to the god Set, and my protector advanced to me, and his face was clothed (or covered), and [he] fell over the hidden things. He entered the Temple of Osiris and looked at the hidden things that were there; and the sovereign chiefs of the pillars [were] in the form of khus. And the god Anpu spoke [to those who were on] both sides of him with the speech of a man [when he] came from Ta-mera; he knows our paths and our cities. I make offerings, and I smell him as if he was one among you, and I tell him, I am Osiris, the scribe Ani, triumphant in peace, triumphant! I came, and (I) got closer to see the great gods, and I feed on the offerings that are among their food. I was on the borders [of the territory of] Ba-neb-Tettet (that is, the 'Soul, the lord of Tattu,' or Osiris), and he made me come forth like a bird Bennu and utter words. I was in the water of the stream and made offerings of incense. I guided myself to the Shentet tree of [divine] children. I was in Abu (that is, Elephantine) in the Temple of the goddess Satet. I submerged the boat of my enemies [while] I myself sailed over the lake in the boat Neshmet. I saw the Sahu (that is, the spiritual bodies) [in] the city of Qem-ur. I was in the city of Tattu, and it brought me to silence [there]. I made the god have the mastery over his two feet. I was in the Temple of Tep-tu-f (that is, 'the one who is on his hill,' or Anubis), and I saw the one who is the lord of the divine temple. I entered the Temple of Osiris and dressed in the clothes of the one who is there. I entered Re-stau and saw the hidden things that are in it. I was wrapped in [it], but I found a path for myself. I went to the city of An-aarret-f (that is, the place where nothing grows), and I covered my nakedness with the garments that were there. It was given to me the ointment [such as] women [use], together with the dust of human beings. In truth, Sut spoke to me the things that concern himself, and I said: 'Let your weighing be in us.'"

"The Majesty of the god Anpu said: 'Do you know the name of this door to declare it to me'? And Osiris, the scribe Ani, triumphant in peace, triumphant! says: 'Destroyer of the god Shu' is the name of this door. The Majesty of the god Anpu said: 'Do you know the name of the upper leaf and the lower leaf?' 'Lord of Maat on his two feet' is the name of the upper leaf, and 'Lord of double strength, the subduer of cattle,' [is the name of the lower leaf. The Majesty of the god Anpu says]: 'Since you know, oh, Osiris, the scribe, the counter of the divine offerings of all the gods of Thebes, Ani, triumphant, the lord of reverence.'"

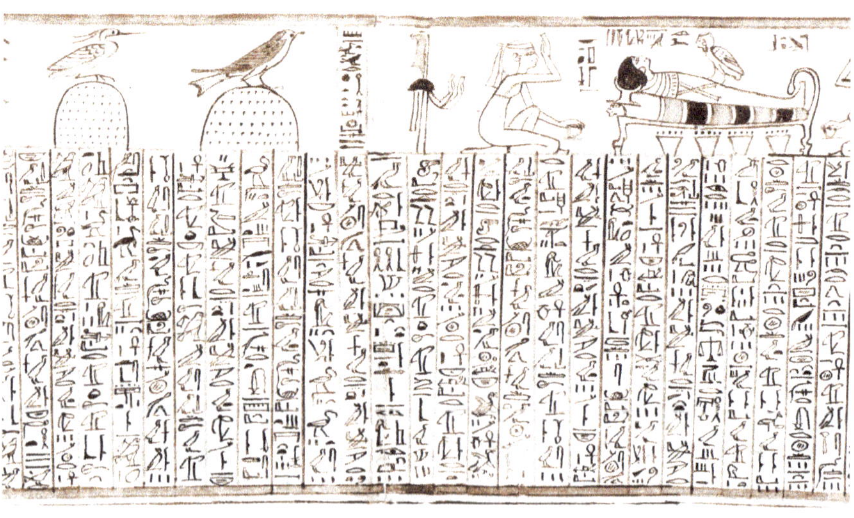

The *Book of the Dead* of Nany.

The Introduction to Maat II

[From the Papyrus of Nu (British Museum N 10477, sheet 22)].

[THE FOLLOWING] WILL BE SAID WHEN THE SUPERIN-TENDENT OF THE PALACE, THE CHANCELLOR-IN-CHIEF, NU, TRIUMPHANT, COMES TO THE HALL OF MAAT, SO THAT HE CAN BE SEPARATED FROM EVERY SIN HE COMMITTED AND CAN SEE THE FACE OF THE GODS. Osiris Nu, triumphant, said:

"Homage to you, O Great God, you Lord of Double Maat, I came to you, oh, my Lord, and I brought myself here so that I may behold your beauties. I know you, and I know your name, and I know the name[s] of the forty-two gods that exist with you in the Hall of Double Maat, which live as guardians of sinners and which feed on their blood on the day when the lives of men are taken into account in the presence of the god Un-nefer; in truth 'Rekhti-merti- neb-Maat' (that is, 'twin sisters with two eyes, ladies of double Maat') is your name. In truth, I came to you and brought Maat (that is, right and truth) to you, and destroyed wickedness for you. [I did not do evil to] humanity. I did not oppress the members of my family; I did not do evil instead of right and truth. I did not have knowledge of useless men. I did not do any harm. I did not make it to be the first [consideration] of every day that excessive work should be done for me. [I] did not present my name for [exaltation] for honors. I did not mistreat servants. [I have not despised a god.] I did not defraud the oppressed one of his goods. I did not do what is an abomination to the gods. I did not harm the servant of his master. I did not cause pain. I did not let any man go hungry. I did not make anyone cry. I did not commit murder. I did not order anyone to commit murder for me. I did not cause pain to humanity. I did not defraud the temples of their oblations. I did not steal the cakes of the gods. I did not take the cakes offered to the khus. I did not commit fornication. I did not pollute myself in the holy places of the god of my city. I did not decrease the bushel. I did not take away or add to the acre measurement. I did not invade [others'] fields. I did not add to the weights of the scales. I did not misread the pointer of the scales. I did not take milk out of the children's mouths. I did not drive the cattle from their pastures. I did not capture the feathered birds from the reserves of the gods. I did not catch fish [with bait made from] fish of its kind. I did not stop the water [when it should flow]. I did not cut a canal dam. I did not extinguish a fire when it should burn. I did not violate the times of [offering] the chosen meat. I did not expel the cattle from the gods' property. I did not repel a god in his appearances. I am pure. I am pure. I am pure. I am pure. My purity is the purity of that great Bennu that is in the city of Suten-henen (Heracleopolis), for, behold, I am the nose of the God of the winds, who makes all humanity live on the day when the Eye (Utchat) of Ra is full in Anu (Heliopolis) at the end of the second month of the Pert season (that is, the season of growth) [in the presence of the divine lord of this land]. I saw the Eye of Ra when it was full in Anu, therefore, do not allow evil to happen to me in this land and in this Hall of the Double Maat, because I, myself, I know the names of these gods that are in it [and who are the followers of the great god]."

The Negative Confession

[From the Papyrus of Nebseni (British Museum N 9900, sheet 30)].

The scribe Nebseni, triumphant, says:

1. Hail, you, the one of long strides, coming before Anu (Heliopolis); I did not commit iniquity.

2. Hail, you, who are surrounded by flame, coming from Kher- aba; I did not steal with violence.

3. Hail, Divine Nose (Fenti), coming before Khmunu (Hermopolis); I did not commit violence [to any man].

4. Hail, you, who eat shadows, coming from the place where the Nile rises; I did not commit theft.

5. Hail, Neha-hau, coming before Re-stau; I did not kill man or woman.

6. Hail, you, double Lion-God, coming before the sky; I did not decrease the bushel.

7. Hail, you, whose two eyes are like flint, coming before Sekhem (Leto-polis); I did not act deceitfully.

8. Hail, you. Flame, coming out as [you] return; I did not steal the things that belong to a god.

9. Hail, you. crusher of bones, coming before Suten-henen (Heracleopolis); I did not utter falsehood.

10. Hail, you, who make the flame grow strong, coming from Het-ka-Ptah (Memphis); I did not take food.

11. Hail, Qerti, (that is, the two sources of the Nile), coming from Amentet; I did not utter evil words.

12. Hail, you, whose teeth shine, coming from Ta-she (that is, the Fayyum); I did not attack any man.

13. Hail, you, who consume blood, coming from the house of slaughter; I did not kill the animals [which are the property of a god].

14. Hail, you, who consume the bowels, coming from the Mabet chamber; I did not act deceitfully.

15. Hail, you, god of Righteousness and Truth, coming from the city of the Double Maat; I did not devastate the lands that were plowed.

16. Hail, you, who walk behind, coming from the city of Bast (Bubastis); I never meddled in matters [to make mischief].

17. Hail, Aati, coming before Anu (Heliopolis); I did not put my mouth in motion [against any man].

18. Hail, you, who are doubly evil, coming from the name of Ati; I did not give place to wrath concerning myself without a cause.

19. Hail, you, serpent Uamemti, coming from the house of slaughter; I did not defile any man's wife.

20. Hail, you, who look at what is brought to him, coming from the Temple of Amsu; I did not commit any sin against purity.

21. Hail, Chief of the divine Princes, coming before the city of Nehatu; I did not cause fear [in any man].

22. Hail, Khemiu (that is, Destroyer), coming from the Lake of Kaui; I did not invade [sacred times and seasons].

23. Hail, you who order speech, coming from Urit; I was not an angry man.

24. Hail, son, coming from the Lake of Heqat; I did not turn a deaf ear to the words of right and truth.

25. Hail, you, who have speech, coming from the city of Unes; I did not provoke strife.

26. Hail, Basti, coming before the secret city; I did not make [any man] cry.

27. Hail, you, whose face is [turned] backwards, coming from the Dwelling; I did not commit acts of impurity, nor slept with men.

28. Hail, leg of fire, coming before Akhekhu; I did not eat my heart.

29. Hail, Kenemti, coming before the [city of] Kenemet; I did not abuse [anyone].

30. Hail, you, who bring your offering, coming from the city of Sau (Sais); I did not act with violence

31. Hail, you, god of faces, coming before the city of Tchavet; I did not judge hastily.

32. Hail, you, who give knowledge, coming from Unth; I did not take revenge on a god.

33. Hail, you, two-horned lord, coming before Satiu; I did not multiply [my] speech.

34. Hail, Nefer-Tem, coming before Het-ka-Ptah (Memphis); I did not act deceitfully, and I did not do evil.

35. Hail, Tem-Sep, coming before Tattu; I did not curse [the king].

36. Hail, you, whose heart aches, coming from the city of Tebti; I did not dirty the water.

37. Hail, Ahi of water, coming before Nu; I did not make my voice haughty.

38. Hail, you, who give orders to humanity, coming from [Sau]; I did not curse a god.

39. Hail, Neheb-nefert, coming from the Lake of Nefer; I did not behave with insolence.

40. Hail, Neheb-kau, coming before [your] city; I did not seek distinctions.

41. Hail, you, whose head is holy, coming from [your] dwellings; I did not increase my wealth, except with the things that are [rightly] my own possessions.

42. Hail, you, who bring your own arm, coming from Aukert (underworld); I did not think to despise the god who is in my city."

Addressing the Gods of the Underworld

[From the Papyrus of Nu (British Museum N 10477, sheet 24)].

[THEN THE HEART THAT IS FAIR AND SINLESS SAYS:]

The superintendent of the palace, the chancellor-in-chief, Nu, triumphant, said:

"Homage to you, oh, gods who dwell in the Hall of Double Maat, I, myself, I know you and know your names. Do not let me fall under your knives of slaughter, and do not present my wickedness to the god on whose train you are; and may no evil come to me through you. Oh, declare me right and true in the presence of Neb-er-tcher, because I did what is right and true in Ta-mera (Egypt). I did not curse a God and I did not let evil come upon me through the king who dwells in my days. Homage to you, oh, gods, who dwell in the Hall of the Double Maat, who have no evil in your bodies, and who live in righteousness and truth, and who feed on righteousness and truth in the presence of the god Horus, who dwells in his divine Disk: deliver me from the god Baba who feeds on the entrails of the mighty ones on the day of the great judgment. Oh, grant me to come to you, for I did not commit faults, I did not sin, I did not do harm, I did not bear false witness; therefore, let nothing [evil] be done to me. I live by right and truth, and I feed of right and truth. I fulfilled the commandments of men [as well as] the things with which the gods are gratified, I made the gods to be in peace [with me by doing] that which is their will. I gave bread to the hungry, and water to the thirsty, and clothing to the naked, and a boat to the [shipwrecked] sailor. I made sacred offerings to the gods and sepulchral meals to the khus. Then be my deliverers, then be my protectors, and do not make accusations against me in the presence of [the great god]. I am clean of mouth and clean of hands; therefore, let those who see me say to me: 'Come in peace; come in peace', for I heard that powerful word which the spiritual bodies (sahu) spoke to the Cat in the House of Hapt-re. I was forced to give testimony before the god Hra-f-ha-f (that is, the one whose face is behind him), and he gave a decision [concerning me]. I saw the things over which the persea tree spreads [its branches] within Re-stau. I am the one who offered prayers to the gods and who knows their people. I came and moved forward to make the declaration

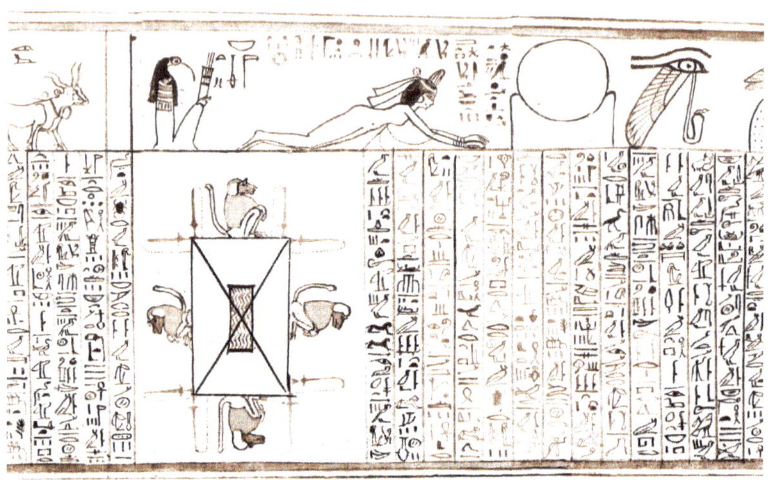

Detail of the Book of the Dead of Nany, singer of Amun.

of right and truth, and to establish the balance that sustains it in the region of Aukert. Hail, you who are exalted on your standard, you lord of the Crown of Atefu, whose name is proclaimed as 'Lord of the Winds,' deliver me from your divine messengers who cause terrible deeds and who cause calamities, and who are without coverings to their faces, for I did what is right and true for the Lord of right and truth. I purified myself and my chest with libations, and my back parts with the things that purify, and my inner parts were in the Lake of Right and Truth. There is not a limb of mine that lacks righteousness and truth. I was purified in the Southern Lake, and I rested in the northern city, which is in the Field of Grasshoppers, where the divine sailors of Ra bathe in the second hour of the night and the third hour of the day. And the hearts of the gods are satisfied after they have passed through it, whether by night or by day, and they say to me: 'Let you come forward.' 'Who, then, are you?' And they say to me: 'What is your name?' 'I am the one who is equipped under the flowers [and I am] the dweller in its olive tree,' that is my name. And they immediately say to me: 'Pass it on;' and I passed through your city north of the olive tree. What, then, did you see there? The leg and the thigh. What, then, did you say to them? Let me see rejoicing in those lands of the Tenkhu. And what did they give you? A flame of fire and a crystal plate (or scepter). What, then, did you do with it? I buried them in the groove of Manaat as 'things for the night.'

What, then, did you find in the groove of Manaat? A flint scepter, whose name is 'Giver of the Winds.' What, then, did you do with the flame of the fire and the crystal plate (or scepter) after you had buried them? I uttered words over them in the groove, [and took them out of there]; I put out the fire, broke the plate (or scepter) and created a puddle of water. 'Come then,' [they say,] 'and enter through the door of this Hall of Double Maat, because you know us.'" "'We will not let you enter through us,' say the bolts on the door, 'unless you tell [us] our names;' 'I will not let you enter through me,' says the [right] lintel of the door, 'unless you tell me my name;' 'I will not let you enter through me,' says the [left] lintel of the door, 'unless you tell me my name;' ['Swing of] wine,' that is your name. 'I will not let you enter through me,' says the threshold of the door, 'unless you tell me my name'; 'Ox of the god Geb,' that is your name. 'I will not open to you,' says the lock of the door, 'unless you tell me my name;' 'Flesh of your mother,' that is your name. 'I will not open to you,' says the hollow of the door's lock, 'unless you tell me my name;' 'Living eye of the god Sobek, the lord of Bakhau,' that is your name. 'I will not open to you [and will not let you enter through me,' says the guardian of the leaf of] this door, 'unless you tell me my name;' 'Elbow of the god Shu when he stands to protect Osiris,' that is your name. 'We will not let you enter through us,' say the frames of the door, 'unless you tell us our name;' 'Sons of the uræi goddesses,' that is your name. 'You know us,' [they say,] 'pass on, therefore, through us.'"

"'I will not let you step on me,' says the floor of the Hall of the Double Maat, 'because I am silent, and I am holy, and because I do not know the name[s] of your two feet with which you want to walk over me; therefore, tell them to me.' 'Traveler of the god Khas,' that is the name of my right foot, and 'Staff of the goddess Hathor,' that is the name of my left foot. 'You know me,' [it says,] 'pass on, therefore, over me.'"

"'I will make no mention of you,' says the guardian of the door of this Double Hall of Maat, 'unless you tell me my name;' 'Now I will make mention of you [to the god]. But who is the god that dwells in your hour? You tell me' (that is, his name). Maau-Taui (that is, the one who keeps the record of the two lands) [that is his name]. 'Who then is Maau-Taui?' He is Thoth. 'Come,' said Thoth. 'But why did you come?' I

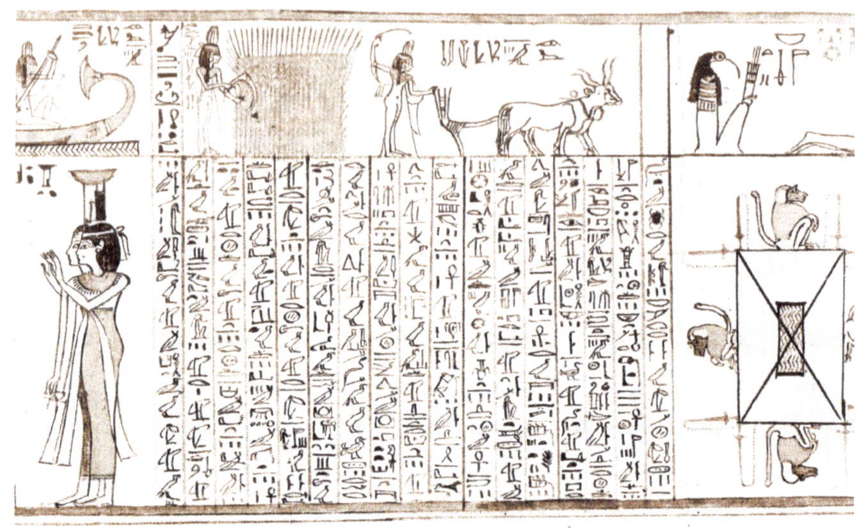

The Book of the Dead of the singer Nany, who died aged around seventy.

came and proceed so that I may be mentioned. What is your condition now? I, myself, I am purified from evil things, and I am protected from the evil deeds of those who live in your days; and I am not among them. 'Now I will make mention of you [to the god].' '[Tell me now,] who is the one whose sky is of fire, whose walls [are surmounted by] living uræi, and the floor of whose house is a stream of water? Who is he,' I say: 'He is Osiris.' 'Come close, then: in truth you will be mentioned [to him]. Your cakes [will come] from the Eye of Ra, and your beer [will come] from the Eye of Ra, and the sepulchral meals [that will be brought to you] on earth [will come] from the Eye of Ra. This was decreed for Osiris, the superintendent of the palace, the chancellor-in-chief, Nu, triumphant.'"

(THE PERFORMANCE OF THE DEPICTION OF WHAT WILL HAPPEN IN THIS HALL OF DOUBLE MAAT.) THIS CHAPTER WILL BE DICTATED [BY THE DEAD] AFTER IT HAS BEEN CLEANSED AND PURIFIED, AND WHEN IT IS DRESSED IN CLOTHING AND SHOE IN WHITE LEATHER SANDALS, AND ITS EYES WERE PAINTED WITH ANTIMONY, AND [ITS BODY] WAS ANOINTED WITH OINTMENT, AND WHEN IT OFFERED OXES, AND FEATHERED BIRDS, AND INCENSE, AND CAKES, AND BEER, AND HERBS OF THE GARDEN. AND BEHOLD, YOU WILL DRAW A DEPICTION OF THESE COLORS ON A NEW CANVAS MOLDED FROM THE EARTH WHICH NEITHER PIGS NOR OTH-

ER ANIMALS HAVE TREADED. AND IF [YOU] MAKE THIS BOOK ABOUT IT [IN WRITING, THE DECEASED] WILL FLOURISH, AND ITS CHILDREN WILL FLOURISH, AND [ITS NAME] WILL NEVER FALL INTO FORGET, AND IT WILL BE LIKE SOMEONE WHO FILLS (I.E., SATISFIES) THE HEART OF THE KING AND HIS PRINCES, AND BREAD, AND CAKES, AND SWEETS, AND WINE, AND PIECES OF MEAT WILL BE GIVEN TO IT ON THE ALTAR OF THE GREAT GOD; AND IT WILL NOT BE RETURNED AT ANY DOOR IN AMENTET, AND IT WILL BE BROUGHT TOGETHER WITH THE KINGS OF UPPER AND LOWER EGYPT, AND IT WILL BE IN THE ENTOURAGE OF OSIRIS CONTINUOUSLY AND REGULARLY FOREVER.

Of the Praise of the Gods

[From the tomb of Ramesses IV (see Naville, op. cit., Bd. I. Bl. 141; Lefébure, "Tombeau de Ramesses IV," Plate 13)].

THE BOOK OF PRAISE OF THE GODS OF QERTI, WHICH A MAN WILL RECITE WHEN HE COMES BEFORE THEM TO ENTER TO SEE THE GOD IN THE GREAT TEMPLE OF THE UNDERWORLD. And he will say:

"Homage to you, oh, gods of Qerti, oh, divine dwellers in Amentet! Homage to you, oh, guardians of the doors of the underworld, who keep the god, who bear and proclaim [the names of those who come] in the presence of the god Osiris, and who stand ready, and who praise [him], and who destroy the Enemies of Ra. Oh, send forth your light and dispel the darkness [that is over] you, and behold the holy and divine Mighty One, oh, you, who live as he lives, and call upon the one who dwells in his divine Disk. Guide the King of the North and the South, (Usr-Maat-Ra-setep-en-Amen), the son of the Sun, (Ra-meses-meri-Amun-Ra-heq-Maat), through your doors, let his divine soul enter into your hidden places, [for] he is one among you, and he cast calamities upon the serpent demon Apep, and he overthrew the obstacles [which Apep established] in Amentet. Your word powerfully prevailed over your enemies, oh, you, great God, who live in your divine Disk; your word prevailed mightily over your enemies, oh, Osiris, Governor of Amentet; your word prevailed mightily over your enemies in heaven and on earth, oh, you,

King of the North and the South, (Usr-Maat-Ra-setep-en-Amen), the son of the Sun, (Ra-meses-meri-Amen-Ra-heq-Maat), and over the sovereign princes of all the gods and all the goddesses, oh, Osiris, Governor of Amentet; he uttered words in the presence [of the god in] the valley of the dead and gained the mastery over the mighty sovereign princes. Hail, gatekeepers, hail, gatekeepers, who keep your gates, who punish souls, who devour the bodies of the dead, who advance upon them in their examination in the places of destruction, who give right and truth to the soul and the divine khu, the beneficent, the mighty one, whose throne is sacred in Akert, who is endowed with soul like Ra and who is praised as Osiris, lead you along the King of the North and the South, (Usr- Maat-Ra-setep-en-Amen), the son of the Sun, (Ra-meses-meri-Amen-Ra-heq-Maat), unlock the doors for him and open [you] the place of your Qerti to him. Hail you, who make your word triumph over your enemies, let meat offerings and drink offerings be made to him by the god of the double gate, and let him put on the crown of Nemes of the one who dwells in the great and hidden sanctuary. Behold the image of Herukhuti (Harmachis), which is doubly true, and which is the divine Soul and the divine and perfect khu; he prevailed with his hands. The two great and mighty gods cry out to the King of the North and the South (Usr- Maat-Ra-setep-en-Amen), the son of the Sun, (Ra-meses-meri-Amen-Ra-heq-Maat), they rejoice with him, they sing praises to him [and clap their hands], they grant him their protection and he lives. The King of the North and the South (Usr-Maat-Ra-setep-en-Amen), the son of the Sun, (Ra-meses-meri-Amen-Ra-heq-Maat), stands like a living soul in heaven. He was ordered to make his transformations, he became victorious before the divine sovereign chiefs and opened the way through the gates of heaven, earth and the underworld, just like Ra. The King of the North and the South (Usr-Maat-Ra-setep-en-Amen), the son of the Sun, (Ra-meses-meri-Amen-Ra-heq-Maat), says: 'Open to me portals of heaven, earth and the underworld, for I am the divine soul of Osiris and I rest in him, and let myself pass through their halls. May [the gods] sing praises to me [when] they see me; let me enter and may grace be given to me; let me come forth and let me be loved; and let me move forward, for no fault or flaw was found in me.'"

Worshipping of the Gods of Qerti

[From the Papyrus of Ptah-mes (Naville, op. cit., Bd. I. Bl. 142)].

A CHAPTER TO BE RECITED WHEN COMING BEFORE THE DIVINE SOVEREIGN CHIEFS OF OSIRIS TO OFFER PRAISE TO THE GODS WHO ARE THE GUIDES OF THE UNDERWORLD. Osiris, the main scribe and draftsman, Ptah-mes, triumphant, said:

"Homage to you, oh, gods who dwell in Qerti, gods who dwell in Amentet, who keep the gates of the underworld and are the guardians [of them], who bear and proclaim [the names of those who come] in the presence of Osiris, who praise him and who destroy the enemies of Ra. Oh, send forth your light and scatter the darkness [that is over] you, and look at the face of Osiris, oh, you, who live as he lives, and praise [you] the one who dwells in his Disk, and guide me away from the calamities. Let me come forth and let me enter through your secret places, for I am a mighty prince among you, for there I put an end to evil and overthrew the obstacles [that were placed] in Amentet. You were victorious over your enemies, oh, you, who dwell in your Disk; you were victorious over your enemies, oh, Thoth, you who create statutes; you were victorious over your enemies, oh, Osiris, the main scribe and draftsman, Ptah-mes, triumphant; you were triumphant over your enemies, oh, Osiris, you, Governor of Amentet, in heaven and on earth in the presence of the divine sovereign chiefs of all the gods and all the goddesses; and the food of Osiris, the governor of Amentet, is in the presence of the god whose name is hidden from the great divine sovereign chiefs. Hail, guardians of the doors, you [gods] who keep your dwellings, who keep the reckoning and who hand over [souls] to destruction, who grant right and truth to the divine soul that is established, that is without evil in the abode of Akert, who are endowed with soul just as Ra, and who are... as is Osiris, guide you Osiris, the main scribe, the draftsman, Ptah-mes, triumphant; open to him the gates of the underworld and the uppermost part of your property and your Qerti. May [he] be victorious over his enemies, provide [him] with the offerings of the god of the underworld, make noble the divine being who dwells in the crown of Nemes, the lord of knowledge of Akert. May this soul be established in righteousness and truth, [and may

The Book of the Dead of Nany; the singer also had the title of Daughter of the King.

it become] a perfect soul that gained the mastery with its two hands. The great and mighty gods cry out: 'He gained victory,' and they rejoice in him, and they assign praise to him with their hands, and they turn their faces to him. The living being is triumphant and is like a living soul that dwells in heaven, and he was commanded to carry out [his] transformations. Osiris triumphed over his enemies, and Osiris, the main scribe and draftsman, Ptah-mes, triumphant, gained victory over his enemies in the presence of the great divine sovereign chiefs who dwell in heaven, and in the presence of the great divine sovereign chiefs who dwell in the earth."

Hymn of Praise to Osiris

[From Lepsius, "Todtenbuch," Bl. 51].

A HYMN OF PRAISE TO OSIRIS. Osiris Auf-ankh, triumphant, says:

"Homage to you, oh, Osiris Un-nefer, triumphant, you son of Nut, you firstborn of Geb, you mighty one who come from Nut, you King in the city of Nifu-ur, you Governor of Amentet, you lord of Abtu (Abydos), you lord of souls, you mighty one of strength, you lord of the Atef crown in Suten-henen, you lord of the divine form in the city of

Nifu-ur, you lord of the tomb, you mighty one of souls in Tattu, you, lord of [sepulchral] offerings, you, whose festivals are many in Tattu. The god Horus exalts his father in every place (or sanctuary), and he joins the goddess Isis and the goddess Nephthys; and the god Thoth recites to him the powerful glorification that are within him, [and that] proceed from his mouth, and the heart of Horus is stronger than that of all the gods. Rise up, then, oh, Horus, son of Isis, and avenge your father Osiris. Hail, oh, Osiris, I came to you; I am Horus and I avenged you, and today I feed on the sepulchral meals of oxen and feathered birds and on all the beautiful things [offered] to Osiris. Rise up, then, oh, Osiris, for I overthrew all your enemies for you, and I took revenge on them for you. I am Horus on this beautiful day of your beautiful rising in your Soul that exalts you together with itself on this day before your divine sovereign princes. Hail, oh, Osiris, your ka came to you and is with you, and you rest in it in your name Ka-Hetep. I make you glorious in your name of khu, and it makes you like the Morning Star in your name of Pehu, and it opens for you the paths in your name of Ap-uat. Hail, oh, Osiris, I came to you and placed your enemies under [your feet] everywhere, and you are triumphant in the presence of the company of the gods and the divine sovereign chiefs. Hail, oh, Osiris,

The Book of the Dead of Nany, singer of Amun.

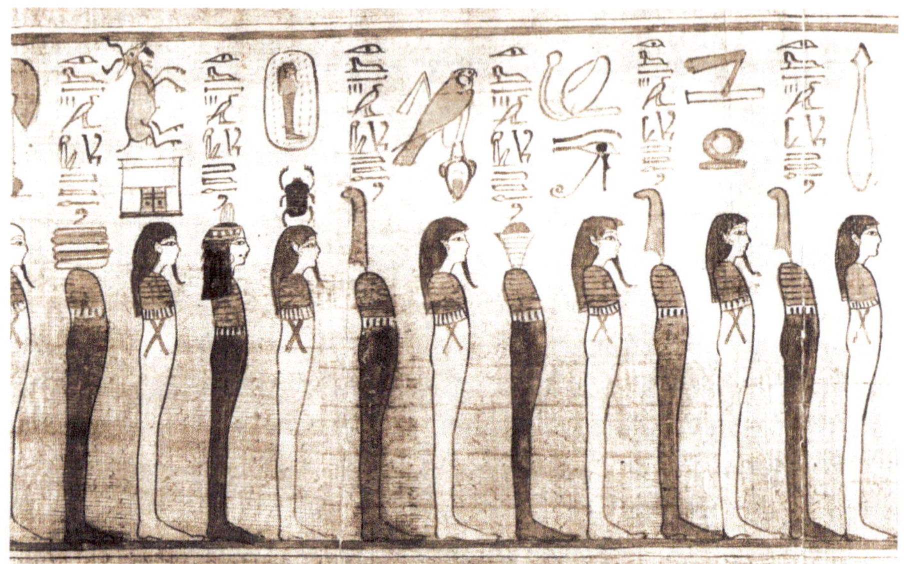

The Book of the Dead of Nany, circa 1040–945 BC.

you received your scepter and the place where you should rest, and your steps are under you. You bring food to the gods, and you bring sepulchral meals to those who dwell in their tombs. You gave your power to the gods, and you created the Great God; you have your existence with them in their spiritual bodies, you gather yourself to all the gods, and you hear the word of right and truth on the day when offerings to this god are commanded in the festivals of Uka."

Of Making Perfect the Khu I

[From the Papyrus of Nu (British Museum N 10477, sheet 17)].

ANOTHER CHAPTER ABOUT MAKING THE KHU PERFECT, WHICH IS [RECITED ON] THE BIRTHDAY OF OSIRIS, AND OF MAKING THE SOUL LIVE FOREVER. The chancellor-in-chief, Nu, triumphant, said:

"The skies are open, the earth is open, the west is open, the east is open, the southern half of the sky is open, the northern half of the sky is open, the doors are open, and the gates are wide open to Ra [when] he appears from the horizon. The boat Sektet opens for him the double doors and the boat Matet opens [for him] the gates; he breathes, and the god Shu [comes into existence], and he creates the goddess Tefnut. Those who follow Osiris follow in his entourage, and the superintendent of the palace, the chancellor-in-chief, Nu, triumphant, goes forward in the entourage of Ra. He takes his iron weapon and opens the sanctuary by force, as well as Horus, and going forward, he advances to the hidden things of his dwelling with the libations of his divine sanctuary; the messenger of the god who loves him. Osiris Nu, the superintendent of the palace, the chancellor-in-chief, triumphant, reveals right and truth, and he makes going forward the advance of Osiris. Osiris Nu, the superintendent of the palace, the chancellor-in-chief, triumphant, takes in [his] hand[s] the rope and he ties the sanctuary. Storms are the things he abhors. May no flood come close to him, may Osiris Nu, the superintendent of the palace, the chancellor-in-chief, triumphant, do not be repelled before Ra, and may he not be compelled to return; for behold, the Eye is in his two hands. May Osiris Nu, the superintendent of the palace, the chancellor-in-chief, triumphant, may he not walk in the valley of darkness, may he not enter the lake of those who are evil; and may he not exist among the damned, even for a moment. Let not Osiris Nu fall head among those who would take him captive, and let not [his] soul enter among them. Let his divine face take possession of the place behind the block, the block of the god Septu."

"Hymns of praise to you, oh, divine beings of the Thigh, the knives of the god [work] in secret, and the two arms and hands of the god make the light shine; it is doubly pleasant for him to lead the old man to him together with the young man at his season. Now, behold, the god Thoth dwells in his hidden places, and he performs the ceremonies of libation for the god who counts millions of years, and he opens a way through the firmament, and he puts an end to the storms and whirlwinds of his fortress, and Osiris Nu, the superintendent of the palace, the chancellor-in-chief, triumphant, arrives in the places of his dwellings. [Oh, divine beings], put an end to his sadness, and his suffering, and his pain, and may the sadness of Osiris Nu be completely removed. Let Osiris Nu, the superintendent of the palace, the chancellor-in-chief, triumphant, gratify Ra, let him make way for the horizon of Ra, let the boat be prepared for him, let him sail happily, and let Thoth put light in [his] heart; then Osiris Nu, triumphant, will praise and glorify Ra, and Ra will listen to his words, and he will overthrow the obstacles that come from his enemies. I did not suffer a shipwreck, I did not return over the horizon, for I am Ra-Osiris, and Osiris Nu, the superintendent of the palace, the chancellor-in-chief, will not shipwreck in the Great Boat. See the one whose face is on the god of the Thigh, because the name of Ra is on the body of Osiris Nu, the superintendent of the palace, the chancellor-in-chief, and his honor is in his mouth; he will talk to Ra, and Ra will listen to his words."

"Hymns of praise to you, oh, Ra, on the horizon, and homage to you, oh, you, who purify with light the dwellers of heaven, oh, you, who have sovereign power over heaven in that supreme moment when the oars of your enemies move! Osiris Nu, the superintendent of the palace, the chancellor-in-chief, triumphant, comes with the order of right and truth, for there is an iron firmament in Amentet that the demon Apep broke with his storms before the double Lion-God, and this will be Osiris Nu set in order; Listen to me, oh, you, who dwell on the top of the throne of majesty. Osiris Nu will enter among your divine sovereign chiefs, and Ra will free you from Apep every day so that it will not approach him, and he will become vigilant. Osiris Nu will have power over the things that are written, he will receive sepulchral meals, and the god Thoth will provide him with the things that must be prepared for him. Osiris Nu does right and true to bypass the arches in the Great Boat, and triumphed among the divine sovereign chiefs, and he established [it] for millions of years. The divine chiefs guide him and give him passage in the boat with joy and happiness; the first ones among the company of sailors of Ra are behind him, and he is happy. Righteousness and truth were exalted and reached their divine lord, and praises were attributed to the god Neb-er-tcher. Osiris Nu, the superintendent of the palace, the chancellor-in-chief, triumphant, took in his hands the weapon and made his way through the sky with it; its dwellers have attributed praise to him as [a] divine being who rises and never sinks to rest. The god Ra exalts him because of what he did and makes him turn the whirlwind and the storm of no effect; he contemplates his splendors and firms his oars, and the boat turns in the sky, rising like the Sun in the darkness. Thoth, the mighty one, leads Osiris Nu within his eye, and he sits [on his] thighs in the mighty boat of Khepera; he comes into existence, and the things he says come to happen. Osiris Nu goes forward, and he travels around the sky to Amentet. The flaming deities rise before him, and the god Shu rejoices greatly, and they take in their hands the arches [of the boat] of Ra together with his divine sailors. Ra turns around and looks at Osiris. Osiris Nu is in peace, Osiris Nu is in peace. He was not repelled, the flame of your moment was not taken away from him; [oh, Ra,] the whirlwind and storm of your mouth did not come against him, he did not travel in the path of the crocodile – for he abhors the crocodile – and he did not come close to it. Osiris Nu boarded your boat, oh, Ra, he is equipped with your throne, and he receives your spiritual form. Osiris Nu travels through the paths of Ra at dawn to repel the demon Nebt; [he] comes over the flame of your boat, [oh, Ra,] over that mighty Thigh. Osiris Nu knows it, and he reaches your boat, and behold, he [sits] in it; and he makes sepulchral offerings."

[THIS CHAPTER WILL BE] RECITED OVER A BOAT OF THE GOD RA THAT WAS PAINTED IN COLORS IN A PURE PLACE. AND BEHOLD, YOU WILL PLACE THE FIGURE OF THE DEAD IN ITS ARCHES, AND YOU WILL PAIN A SEKTET BOAT ON THEIR RIGHT SIDE, AND AN ATET BOAT ON THEIR LEFT SIDE, AND THERE WILL BE AN OFFERING OF BREAD, AND CAKES, AND WINE, AND OIL, AND EVERY KIND OF FAIR OFFERING ON THE BIRTHDAY OF OSIRIS. IF THESE CEREMONIES ARE PERFORMED, THEIR SOULS WILL CONTINUE TO EXIST, AND THEY WILL LIVE FOREVER, AND WILL NOT DIE A SECOND TIME.

The following is from the rubric of this chapter in the Saite Recension (see Lepsius, "Todtenbuch", Bl. 53):

"[He must know] the hidden things of the underworld, he must penetrate the hidden things in Neter-khertet (the underworld)."

"[This chapter] was found in the great hall of the Temple under the reign of his Majesty Hesepti, triumphant, and it was found in the cavern of the mountain that Horus made for his father Osiris Un-nefer, triumphant. Now, as Ra sees this deceased in his own flesh, he will see it as the companion of the gods. The fear of it will be great, and its reverence will be powerful in the hearts of men, and gods, and khus, and the damned. It will be with his soul and live forever; it will not die a second time in the underworld; and on the day of weighing the words, no harm will come to it. It will be triumphant over its enemies, and its sepulchral meals will be over the altar of Ra in the course of each day, day after day."

Of Making Perfect the Khu II

[From the Papyrus of Nu (British Museum N 10477, sheet 16)].

THE BOOK OF MAKING THE KHU PERFECT, WHICH MUST BE RECITED ON THE DAY OF THE MONTH. Osiris Nu, the superintendent of the palace, the chancellor-in-chief, triumphant, said:

"Ra rises on his horizon, and his company of gods follows him. The god comes forth of his hidden dwellings and food falls from the eastern horizon of the sky with the word of the goddess Nut, who makes clear the paths of Ra, after which the Prince immediately turns around. Arise then, oh, you, Ra, who dwells in your divine sanctuary, draw to you the winds, inhale the north wind, swallow the skin of your net on the day you breathe right and true. You separate the divine followers and sail in [your] boat to Nut; the divine princes march in front of your word. You count your bones, gather your limbs, turn your face to the beautiful Amentet, and you come, being renewed every day. Behold, you are that Image of Gold, and you possess the splendors of the disks of the sky, and you are terrible; you come, renewing yourself every day. Hail, the horizon rejoices, and there are shouts of joy in the rigging [of your boat]; when the gods who dwell in heaven see Osiris Nu, the superintendent of the palace, the chancellor-in-chief, triumphant, they assign to him, as his due, praises which are similar to those assigned to Ra. Osiris Nu, the superintendent of the palace, the chancellor-in-chief, triumphant, is a divine prince and he seeks the Uraeus crown of Ra, and he, the only one, is strong in good fortune in that supreme body which is one of those divine beings who are in the presence of Ra. Osiris Nu is strong both on earth and in the underworld; and Osiris Nu is strong as Ra every day. Osiris Nu should not take too long, and he must not remain motionless in this land forever. Being doubly beautiful, [he] will see with his two eyes and hear with his two ears; rightly and truly, rightly and truly. Osiris Nu is similar to Ra, and he sets in order the oars [of his boat] among those who are in the entourage of Nu. He does not tell what he saw and does not repeat what he heard in the secret places. Hail, let there be shouts of joy to Osiris Nu, who is of the divine body of Ra, as he travels over Nu, and who propitiates the ka of the god with that which he loves. Osiris Nu, the superintendent of the palace, the chancellor-in-chief, is a falcon whose transformations are powerful (or multiple)."

[THIS CHAPTER WILL BE] RECITED OVER A BOAT FOUR CUBITS LONG AND MADE OF GREEN PORCELAIN [ON WHICH WERE PAINTED] THE DIVINE SOVEREIGN CHIEFS OF THE CITIES; AND A SKY WITH ITS STARS [ALSO] SHALL BE MADE, AND THIS YOU SHALL HAVE MADE CEREMONIALLY PURE BY MEANS OF NATRON AND INCENSE. AND BEHOLD, YOU WILL MAKE AN IMAGE OF RA IN YELLOW ON A NEW PLATE AND PUT IT AT THE BOW OF THE BOAT. AND BEHOLD, YOU WILL PLACE AN IMAGE OF THE KHU THAT YOU WANT TO MAKE PERFECT [AND PLACE] IN THIS BOAT, AND YOU WILL MAKE IT TO TRAVEL IN THE BOAT [WHICH WILL BE MADE IN THE FORM OF THE BOAT] OF RA; AND IT WILL SEE THE GOD RA THEREIN. DO NOT LET THE EYE OF ANY MAN LOOK AT IT, EXCEPT YOUR OWN, OR YOUR FATHER'S, OR YOUR SON'S, AND KEEP [THIS] VERY CAREFULLY. [NOW THESE THINGS] WILL MAKE THE KHU PERFECT IN THE HEART OF RA, AND WILL GIVE IT POWER WITH THE COMPANY OF THE GODS; AND THE GODS WILL SEE IT AS A DIVINE BEING SIMILAR TO THEMSELVES; AND HUMANITY AND THE DEAD WILL LOOK AT IT AND FALL ON THEIR FACES, AND IT WILL BE SEEN IN THE UNDERWORLD IN THE FORM OF THE RADIANCE OF RA.

Of Making Perfect the Khu III

[From the Papyrus of Nu (British Museum N 10477, sheet 17)].

ANOTHER CHAPTER OF MAKING THE KHU PERFECT. Osiris Nu, the superintendent of the palace, the chancellor-in-chief, triumphant, said:

"Homage to you, oh, you, who are within your divine sanctuary, who shine with rays of light and send forth splendor from yourself, who decree joy for millions of years to those who love you, who give

Binding of the Book of the Dead of Neferiou.

Detail of the binding of the Book of the Dead of Neferiou,
showing the Ba visiting the tomb.

the wish of their hearts to humanity, you, god Khepera, inside your boat that overthrew Apep. Oh, children of the god Geb, overthrow the enemies of Osiris Nu, the superintendent of the palace, the chancellor-in-chief, triumphant, and destroy them from the boat of Ra; and the god Horus will cut off their heads in heaven [where they are] in the form of feathered birds, and their hind parts will be on the earth in the form of animals and in the lake in the form of fish. Every male demon and every female demon must Osiris Nu, the superintendent of the palace, the chancellor-in-chief, destroy; if they descend from the sky, or if they come out of the earth, or if they come upon the waters, or if they advance towards the stars, the god Thoth, the son of Aner, coming from Anerti, will cut them into pieces. Osiris Nu is silent; may this god, the mighty one of slaughter, being greatly feared, clean himself in their blood and bathe in their blood, and they will certainly be destroyed by him from the boat of his father Ra. Osiris Nu is the god Horus to whom his mother, the goddess Isis gave birth, and whom the goddess Nephthys nursed and lulled, as well as Horus when [he] repelled the demons of the god Suti; and when they see the Uraeus crown established on his head, they fall down on their faces and glorify him.

Behold, when men, and gods, and khus, and the dead see Osiris Nu in the form of Horus with the Uraeus crown established on his head, they fall on their faces. And Osiris Nu, the superintendent of the palace, the chancellor-in-chief, triumphant, is victorious over his enemies in the heights of heaven, and in the depths thereof, and before the divine sovereign chiefs of all the gods and all the goddesses."

[THIS CHAPTER] WILL BE RECITED OVER A STANDING FALCON WITH THE WHITE CROWN ON HIS HEAD, [AND OVER FIGURES OF] TEM, SHU, TEFNUT, GEB, NUT, OSIRIS, ISIS, SUTI AND NEPHTHYS PAINTED IN YELLOW ON A NEW PLATE, WHICH WILL BE PLACED ON THE [MODEL OF] THE BOAT [OF THE SUN], TOGETHER WITH THE FIGURE OF THE DEAD WHOM YOU WANT TO MAKE PERFECT. YOU SHALL ANOINT THESE WITH CEDAR OIL, AND INCENSE SHALL BE OFFERED TO THEM IN THE FIRE, AND THE FEATHERED BIRDS WILL BE ROASTED. IT IS AN ACT OF PRAISE TO RA AS HE TRAVELS, AND IT WILL MAKE A MAN TO BE TOGETHER WITH RA DAY BY DAY WHEREVER THE GOD TRAVELS; AND IT WILL DESTROY THE ENEMIES OF RA REGULARLY AND CONTINUOUSLY.

Of Making Perfect the Khu IV

[From the Papyrus of Nu (British Museum N 10477, sheet 16)].

ANOTHER CHAPTER OF MAKING THE KHU PERFECT; [it must be recited] at the festival of Six. Osiris Nu, the superintendent of the palace, the chancellor-in-chief, triumphant, said:

"Behold now, oh, you, luminaries in Anu (Heliopolis), you, people in Kher-aba, the god is born; his rope was completed, and the instrument with which he makes his way he grasped firmly; and Osiris Nu is strong with them to direct the implement of the gods. Osiris Nu delivered the boat of the sun with this... and he came forth to the sky. Osiris Nu sailed in the sky, he traveled to Nut, he traveled together with Ra, and he traveled there in the form of monkeys; [he] turned back the flood that was on the Thigh of the goddess Nut on the staircase of the god Sebaku. The hearts of Geb and Nut rejoice and repeat the name that is new. Un-neferu renews [his] youth, Ra is in his splendors of light, Unti has his speech, and behold, the god of the Flood is the Prince among the gods. The taste of sweetness forced a way into the heart of the helpless, and the lord of your cries was eliminated, and the oars of the company of the gods are in vigorous motion. May you be worshiped, oh, divine Soul, who are endowed more than the gods of the South and the North [in] their splendors! Behold, grant you that Osiris Nu may be great in heaven as well as you are great among the gods; deliver him from every evil and murderous thing that may be wrought upon him by the Evil One, and strengthen his heart. Grant you, moreover, that Osiris Nu may be stronger than all the gods, all the khus, and all the dead. Osiris Nu is strong and is the lord of powers. Osiris Nu is the lord of right and truth, that the goddess Uatchit works. The strength that protects Osiris Nu is the strength that protects the god Ra in the sky. Oh, god Ra, grant that Osiris Nu may travel in your boat in peace, and prepare a path on which [your] boat may go forward; for the strength that protects Osiris is the strength that protects you. Osiris Nu repels the Crocodile from Ra day by day. Osiris Nu comes as well as Horus in the splendors of the horizon of the sky, and he directs Ra through the mansions of the sky. The gods rejoice greatly when Osiris Nu repels the Crocodile. Osiris Nu has the amulet of the god, and the cloud of Nebt will not come close to him, and the divine guardians of the mansions of the sky will not destroy him. Osiris Nu is a divine being whose face is hidden, and he dwells within the Great House [as] the chief of the Sanctuary of the god. Osiris Nu takes the words of the gods to Ra, and he comes and makes supplications to the divine lord with the words of his message. Osiris Nu is strong of heart, and he makes his offering at the moment among those who perform the ceremonies of sacrifice."

[THIS CHAPTER] WILL BE DICTATED OVER THE FIGURE OF THE DEAD THAT WILL BE PLACED IN THE [MODEL OF] THE BOAT OF THE SUN, AND BEHOLD, [THE ONE WHO RECITES IT] WILL BE WASHED AND WILL BE CEREMONIALLY PURE, AND IT WILL HAVE BURNT INCENSE BEFORE RA, AND SHALL OFFER WINE, AND CAKES AND ROASTED BIRDS FOR THE JOURNEY [OF THE DEAD] IN THE BOAT OF RA. NOW, EVERY KHU FOR WHOM SUCH THINGS ARE DONE SHALL HAVE AN EXISTENCE AMONG

THE LIVING, AND IT WILL NEVER PERISH, AND IT WILL HAVE A BEING LIKE THAT OF A HOLY GOD; NO EVIL THING WILL ATTACK IT. AND IT WILL BE LIKE A HAPPY KHU IN AMENTET, AND IT WILL NOT DIE A SECOND TIME. IT WILL EAT AND DRINK IN THE PRESENCE OF OSIRIS EVERY DAY; IT WILL BE CARRIED ALONG WITH THE KINGS OF THE NORTH AND THE SOUTH EVERY DAY; IT WILL DRINK WATER FROM THE SPRING; IT WILL COME FORTH BY DAY AS HORUS; IT WILL LIVE AND BECOME LIKE A GOD; AND IT WILL BE HYMNED BY THE LIVING, AS WELL AS RA EVERY DAY CONTINUOUSLY AND REGULARLY FOREVER.

Of Living Close to Ra

[From the Papyrus of Nu (British Museum N 10477, sheets 17 and 18)].

THE CHAPTER OF HAVING CLOSE EXISTENCE TO RA. The superintendent of the palace, the chancellor-in-chief, Nu, triumphant, said:

"I am that god Ra who shines in the night. Every being who follows him will have life following the god Thoth, and he will give him the ancestries of Horus in the darkness. The heart of Osiris Nu, the superintendent of the palace, the chancellor-in-chief, triumphant, is happy because he is one of these beings, and his enemies were destroyed by the divine princes. I am a follower of Ra and [received] his iron weapon. I came to you, oh, my father Ra, and moved forward to the god Shu. I cried out to the mighty goddess, equipped the god Hu, and I removed the god Nebt from the path of Ra. I am a Khu and I came to the divine prince on the edge of the horizon. I met and received the powerful goddess. I raised up your soul by following your strength and my soul [lives] through your victory and your great power; I am the one who give orders out loud to Ra in the sky. Homage to you, oh, great god in the east of the sky, let me board in your boat; oh, Ra, let me open myself in the form of a divine falcon, let me give my commands in words, let me fight in my Sekhem, let me be the master under my vine. Let me board in your boat, oh, Ra, in peace, and let me sail in peace to the beautiful Amentet. May the god Tem talk to me, [saying], 'Do [you] want to enter there?' The lady, the goddess Mehen, is a million years old, yes, two million years old, and lives in the House of Urt and Nif-urt [and in] the Lake of a Million Years; the whole company of the gods move among those who are on the side of the one who is the lord of the divisions of places. And I say: 'On all the roads and among these millions of years is Ra, the lord, and his path is in the fire, and they turn after him, and they turn after him'".

Of Bringing Men Back to Earth

[From the Papyrus of Ani (British Museum N 10470, sheet 18)].

THE CHAPTER OF BRINGING A MAN BACK TO EARTH TO SEE HIS HOUSE. Osiris Ani says:

"I am the Lion-God arising with long strides. I shot arrows and wounded the prey; I shot arrows and wounded the prey. I am the Eye of Horus, and I pass through the Eye of Horus in this season. I reached the grooves; let Osiris Ani move forward in peace."

The judgment of Osiris, a central element of the funerary papyri.

Excerpt of the *Book of the Dead* of Nodjmet.

For the New Moon

[From Lepsius, "Todtenbuch," Bl. 55].

ANOTHER CHAPTER TO BE RECITED WHEN THE MOON RENEWS ITSELF ON THE DAY OF THE MONTH. Osiris Auf-ankh, triumphant, says:

"Osiris unchains", or, as others say, "opens the storm cloud [in] the body of heaven, and he himself is unhindered; Horus becomes strong and happy every day. The one whose transformations are great (or many) has offerings made to him at the moment, and they put an end to the storm that is on the face of Osiris Auf-ankh, triumphant. In truth he comes, and he is Ra in [his] journey, and he is the four heavenly gods in heaven above. Osiris Auf-ankh, triumphant, comes forth in his day, and he boards among the tackle of the boat."

IF THIS CHAPTER IS KNOWN BY THE DEAD, IT WILL BECOME A PERFECT KHU IN THE UNDERWORLD, AND IT WILL NOT DIE THERE A SECOND TIME, AND IT WILL EAT ITS FOOD SIDE BY SIDE WITH OSIRIS. IF THIS CHAPTER IS KNOWN BY THE DEAD ON EARTH, IT WILL BE LIKE THOTH AND WILL BE WORSHIPED BY THE LIVING; IT WILL NOT FALL HEAD AT THE MOMENT OF THE ROYAL FLAME OF THE GODDESS BAST, AND THE MIGHTY PRINCESS WILL MAKE IT ADVANCE HAPPILY.

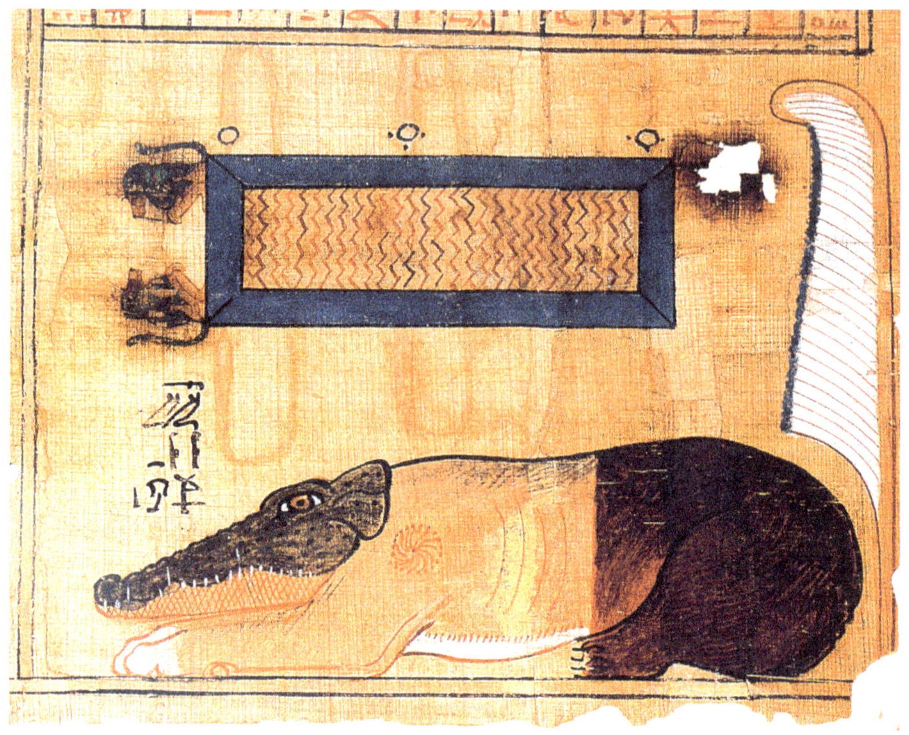

One of the first images of Ammit, who devours damned souls in the afterlife (detail in a *Book of the Dead*).

Of Traveling in the Boat of Ra

[From the Papyrus of Nu (British Museum N 10477, sheet 28)].

ANOTHER CHAPTER OF TRAVELLING IN THE GREAT BOAT OF RA. Osiris Nu, the superintendent of the palace, the chancellor-in-chief, triumphant, said:

"Behold now, oh, luminaries in Anu, oh, people in Kher-aba, the god Kha is born; his rope was completed and the instrument with which he makes his way [he] grasped firmly. I protected the implements of the gods and handed over the boat Kha to him. I came to heaven and traveled there with Ra in the form of a monkey, and returned the ways of Nut on the ladder of the god Sobek."

Sailing in the Great Boat

[From the Papyrus of Nu (British Museum N 10477, sheet 28)].

THE CHAPTER OF SAILING THE GREAT BOAT OF RA TO PASS OVER THE CIRCLE OF BRIGHT FLAME. Osiris Nu, the superintendent of the palace, the chancellor-in-chief, triumphant, said:

"[Hail], oh, bright and shining flames that keep your place behind Ra, and that kill behind him, the boat of Ra is afraid of the whirlwind and the storm; shine, then, and become visible. I came [daily] together with the god Sek-hra from the bay of his sacred lake, and saw the Maat [goddesses] pass by, and the lion-gods that belong to them. Hail, you who dwell in the vault that has multitudes of plants, I saw [what is] there. We rejoice, and your princes rejoice greatly, and your lesser gods are glad. I made a way in front of the boat of Ra, I lifted myself in his divine disk, I shined through his splendors; he provided himself with the things that are his, taking possession of them as the lord of right and truth. And behold, oh, company of the gods, and you, ancestor of the goddess Isis, grant that he may bear

Part of the *Book of the Dead* of the scribe Nebqed, who lived during the reign of Amenophis III (1391–1353 BC), 18th dynasty. Followed by his mother Amenemheb and his wife Meryt, Nebqed encounters the Egyptian god of the dead, Osiris.

witness of his father, the lord of those who are therein. I weighed the heart on him [as] chief, and I brought to him the goddess Tefnut and he lives. Behold, come, come and declare before him the testimony of the righteousness and truth of the Lord Tem. I cry out at the evening and at its hour, saying: Grant me that I may go. I brought him the jaws of the passages of the tomb; I brought him the bones that are in Anu (Heliopolis); I gathered for him his multiple parts; I expelled for him the demonic serpent Apep; I spat on his cuts for him; I made my way and passed among you. I am the one who dwells among the gods, come, let me pass in the boat, the boat of Lord Sa. Behold, oh, Heru-ur, there is a flame, but the fire was extinguished. I made [my] road, oh, divine parents and your divine monkeys! I entered the horizon and passed to the side of the divine princes and bore witness to the one who dwells in his divine boat. I moved forward over the circle of bright flame that is behind the lord of the lock of hair that moves around. Behold, you who cry out over yourselves, oh, worms in [your] hidden places, grant me that I may go forward, for I am the mighty one, the lord of divine strength, and I am the spiritual body (sahu) of the lord of divine right and truth made by the goddess Uatchit. Your strength that protects is my strength that protects, which is the strength that protects Ra. [Grant that I may follow Ra], and grant that I may walk with him in Sekhet-Hetepet [and in] the two lands. [I am] a great god, and [I was] judged by the company of your gods; grant that divine and sepulchral meals may be given to me."

Of the Four Flames

[From the Papyrus of Nu (British Museum N 10477, sheet 26)].

THE CHAPTER OF THE FOUR BRIGHT FLAMES WHICH
ARE MADE FOR THE KHU. Behold, you will make four square troughs of clay, on which you will spread incense, and you will fill them with the milk of a white cow, and through them, you will extinguish the flame. Osiris Nu, the superintendent of the palace, the chancellor-in-chief, triumphant, said:

"Fire comes to your ka, oh, Osiris, governor of Amenti; fire comes to your ka, oh, Osiris Nu, the superintendent of the palace, the chancellor-in-chief, triumphant. The one who orders the night comes after the day. [The flame comes to your ka, oh, Osiris, governor of those in Amenti] and the two sisters of Ra come in the same way. Behold, [the flame] arises in Abtu (Abydos) and comes; and I cause it to come [to] the Eye of Horus. It is set in order on your forehead, oh, Osiris, governor of Amenti, and it is fixed within your sanctuary and rises upon your forehead; it is placed in order on your chest, oh, Osiris Nu, and it is fixed on your forehead. The Eye of Horus is protecting you, oh, Osiris, governor of Amenti, and it keeps you safe; it overthrows all your enemies headlong for you, and all your enemies fell head down before you. Oh, Osiris Nu, the Eye of Horus protects you, keeps you safe, and overthrows all your enemies headlong. Your enemies fell headlong before your ka, oh, Osiris, governor of Amenti, the Eye of Horus protects you, keeps you safe, and overthrows all your enemies headlong. Your enemies fell headlong before your ka, oh, Osiris Nu, the superintendent of the palace, the chancellor-in-chief, triumphant, the Eye of Horus protects you, it keeps you safe, overthrew headlong

The Weighing of the Heart of the *Book of the Dead* of Ani: on the left, Ani and his wife Tutu enter the assembly of the gods.

for you all your enemies, and your enemies fell headlong before you. The Eye of Horus comes, it is good and healthy, and it sends rays like Ra on the horizon; it covers with darkness the powers of Suti, takes possession of them, and brings its flame against him upon [his] feet. The Eye of Horus is healthy and good, you eat the flesh of your body through it, and you give praise to it. The four flames enter your ka, oh, Osiris, governor of Amenti, the four flames enter your ka, oh, Osiris Nu, the superintendent of the palace, the chancellor-in-chief, triumphant. Hail, sons of Horus, Imsety, Hapi, Duamutef and Qebehsenuef, you gave your protection to your divine father Osiris, the governor of Amenti, grant your protection to Osiris Nu, triumphant. Now therefore, since you destroyed the opponent[s] of Osiris, the governor of Amenti, he lives with the gods, and he hurt Suti, with his hand and arm since the light dawned upon the earth, and Horus got power, and he himself avenged his divine father Osiris; and since your divine father became vigorous through the union you carried out for him with the ka of Osiris, the governor of Amenti – now the Eye of Horus avenged him, and protected him, and overthrew headlong for him all his enemies, and all his enemies fell before him -

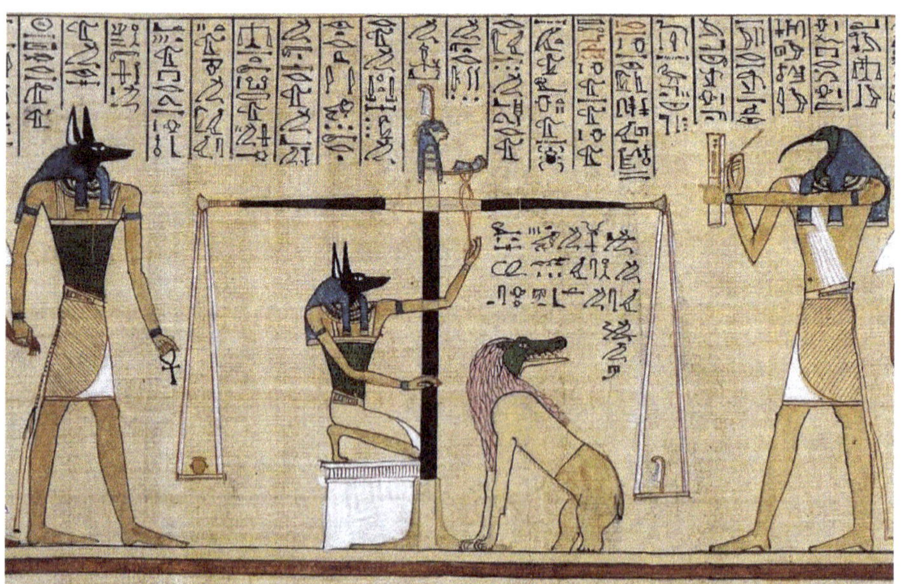

Vignette of the *Book of the Dead* of Hunefer.

even so, destroy the opponent[s] of Osiris Nu, the superintendent of the palace, the chancellor-in-chief, triumphant. Let him live with the gods, let him hurt his enemy, let him destroy him when light dawns upon the earth, let Horus gain power and avenge Osiris Nu, let Osiris Nu have vigor through the union you carried out for him with his ka. Oh, Osiris Nu, the Eye of Horus avenged you, he overthrew all your enemies headlong for you, and all your enemies fell headlong before you. Hail, Osiris, governor of Amenti, grant light and fire to the happy soul that is in Suten-henen (Heracleopolis); and [oh, sons of Horus] grant power to the living soul of Osiris Nu within his flame. May he not be repelled and not be rejected at the doors of Amentet; oh, let the offerings of bread and linen garments be brought to him among [those of] the lords of funeral oblations, oh, offer praises as to a god, to the Osiris Nu, destroyer of his opponent[s] in his form of righteousness and truth and in his attributes of a god of righteousness and truth."

Papyrus of the Book of the Dead of Pinedjem II, who makes an offering to the god Osiris.

CHECK OUT OUR
RELEASES HERE!

Camelot
EDITORA